20
HOT POTATOES
CHRISTIANS ARE
AFRAID TO
TOUCH

Also by Anthony Campolo

Partly Right
A Reasonable Faith
It's Friday, but Sunday's Comin'
You Can Make a Difference
Who Switched the Price Tags?

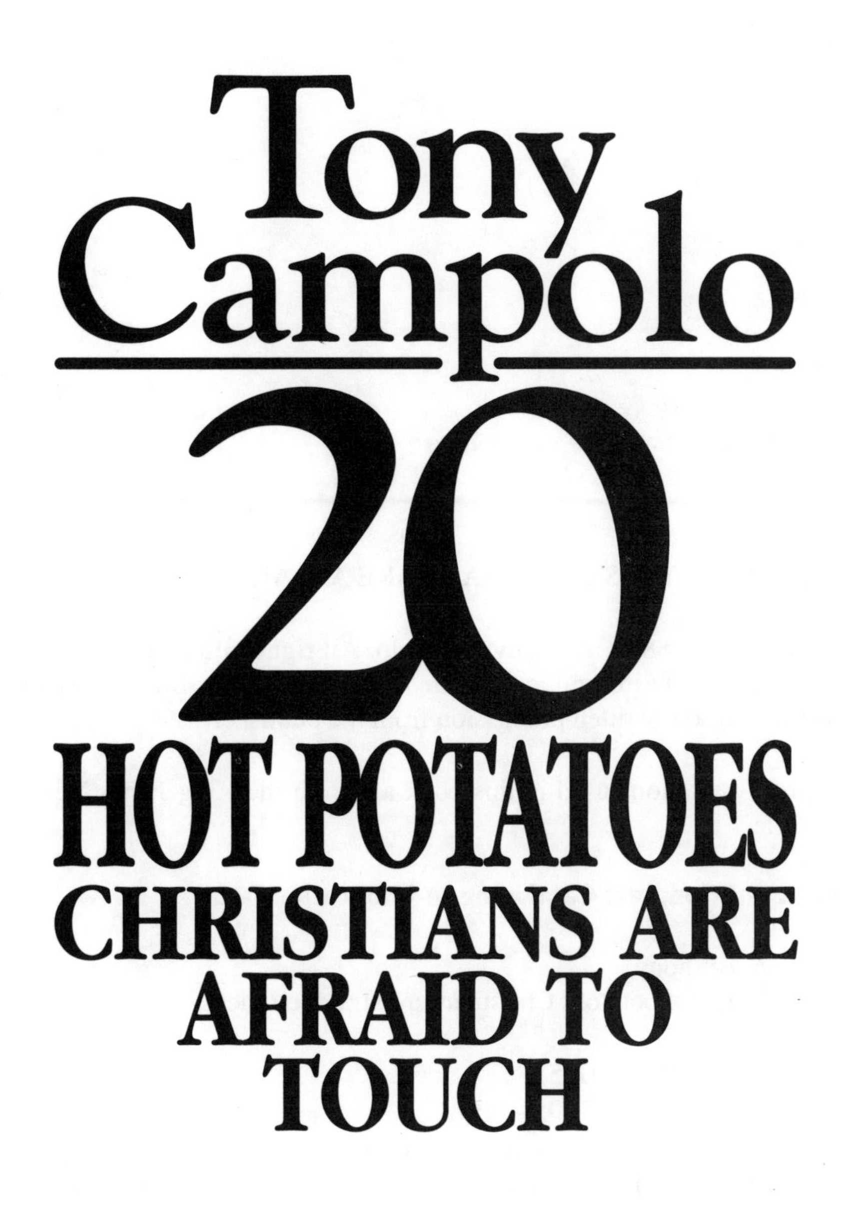
Tony Campolo

20 HOT POTATOES CHRISTIANS ARE AFRAID TO TOUCH

WORD PUBLISHING
Dallas · London · Vancouver · Melbourne

20 HOT POTATOES CHRISTIANS ARE AFRAID TO TOUCH

Scripture quotations used in this book are from the King James Version of the Bible.

Library of Congress Cataloging-in-Publication Data:

Campolo, Anthony.
Twenty hot potatoes Christians are afraid to touch.
p. cm.
ISBN 0–8499–0655–5
0–8499–3505–9 (pbk.)
1. Christian ethics—Baptist authors. 2. Social ethics.
I. Title. II. Title: Twenty hot potatoes Christians are afraid to touch.
BJ1251.C25 1988 241 88–26173
CIP

Printed in the United States of America

3 4 5 6 7 8 9 LBM 17 16 15 14

To Lisa Davidson Campolo

A very good lawyer,
A very bright philosopher,
And my very own daughter.

Contents

Introduction

WHEN I WAS A PASTOR, I was a bit cautious about what I preached. I tried to be prophetic and preach the hard things that people needed to hear, but I am not sure I did it well. A pastor has to keep his people with him or her, and preaching too many controversial sermons makes that difficult, if not impossible. Consequently, there were a lot of things I feel I should have said that I did not say, and there were a lot of things I said that I wished I had not.

Years have passed, and I have grown bolder and less cautious. Perhaps my increased daring stems from the fact that I no longer have a Sunday morning congregation. Or maybe I am a bit bolder because, having crossed the fifty-year-old mark, I do not care quite as much as I once did about "making it" in my career. Then again, it just may be that I am coming to realize that an honest preacher does not hold back, but shares what God has laid on his or her heart.

Regardless of the reason or reasons, I feel that the time has come to be bold and to declare from the rooftops what I have been hiding away in my closet of opinions. The time has come to talk about many important things that perhaps I should have talked about a long time ago.

The range of topics in this book is wide. I hope I have dealt with topics that vitally concern you. While I know that much of what I have said in this book may be controversial, I did not write it because I *wanted* to be controversial or to make people angry. I just wanted to deal with some crucial issues that are seldom handled from the pulpit. I wanted to speak to such sensitive topics as homosexuality and divorce. I wanted to offer my ideas on heavy issues such as the ordination of women and our attitudes toward AIDS victims. I wanted to speak out strongly on some of my own pet peeves, such as hunting and overpriced funerals. And I wanted to share what I know for those people who have personal problems that cause them to feel the need for psychotherapy, and for those who are beside themselves with worry because their grownup children are so messed up.

In all that I have written, I have tried to maintain a high regard for Scripture on the one hand and a deep empathy for the people involved in these problems on the other. I have written with the hope of helping many and of angering as few as possible. My great fear is that I may end up only helping a few and angering many. But even if the latter is the case, I honestly feel that the book was worth writing. The angry will get over their anger and, in the end, will think less only of me. And I believe that their displeasure with me is a small price to pay if I help even a few.

I am a relatively helpless person when it comes to turning out books. So for producing this volume, I must give special credit to the competent and caring women in my office—Mary Noel Keough, Pat Carroll, and Sue Dahlstrom. My thanks also to Kim Feeser and to Peggy Carlson. A special thank-you goes to my efficient and sympathetic editor at Word Books, Anne Christian Buchanan.

But most of all, I have to get down on my knees and offer homage to my wife. She is the one who really made this book happen. She corrected the spelling and the grammar, critiqued the ideas, and kept me honest enough to say what I really believe. Her name is Peggy, and I love her very much.

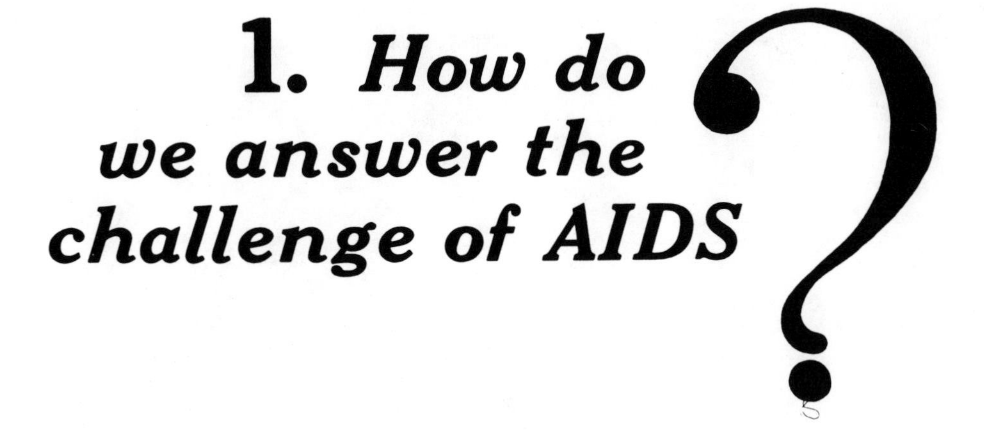
1. How do
we answer the
challenge of AIDS

A COUPLE OF YEARS AGO, I was invited to conduct an evangelistic crusade in Sacramento, California. It was a wonderful experience for me. There were four evening meetings scheduled to take place at the Arco Arena. The same organizing committee that had put together the highly successful Billy Graham Crusade a couple of years earlier did all the things that are supposed to be done to insure that proper preparations were made. For a sociology professor at a small liberal arts college this was all pretty heady stuff.

The first night of the crusade was great. The Arco Arena was filled. The music was perfect, and the program unfolded without a hitch. Following the sermon, when the invitation to "decide for Christ" was given, there was a good response.

The next morning, the planning committee for the crusade had a meeting to review how things had gone and to see if there were any improvements that needed to be made. Everyone was quite euphoric about the previous night's meeting except for the person in charge of publicity and public relations. He was a little down because the meeting had gotten no coverage in the Sacramento newspapers or on the local television stations. In his opinion, the meetings were entitled to some media coverage, especially in light of the fact that more than ten thousand people had been in attendance.

I tried to comfort him by pointing out that filling the arena was no big deal to those people who put together news stories. I noted that the Arco Arena gets filled a couple of times every week—the place packs out with great regularity for rock concerts and professional basketball games. It was not prejudice against religion that had led the media to ignore us, I explained. Rather, it was the fact that filling the Arco Arena for a religious meeting is not the sort of thing that makes for a great public interest story.

Then, in the inspiration of the moment, I added, "If you really want to get the media here, I can tell you how to do it. But we have to do something more than fill the arena with a bunch of hymn singers to pull it off."

The committee was all ears.

"Why not designate an offering tomorrow night to go for people in Sacramento who are suffering from AIDS? Those who come down with that disease need all the help that they can get. If a bunch of evangelicals reach out in love to AIDS victims, most of whom are homosexuals, that's news!"

The committee bought it. They already had the money they needed to cover the expenses for the crusade, so they could afford to be generous. Besides, the idea appealed to them. The meetings were being held the same week as the first International Conference on AIDS, so the subject of AIDS was "hot" to the press. So we sent notices of what would be done with the offering to the various newspapers and television stations of the city, and we all waited with great anticipation to see what the reaction would be.

When I got to the arena that night, my expectations were more than realized. In addition to the reporters from the local papers, there were camera crews from each of the three network TV stations. These media people remained immobile, and no cameras were turned on all during the song service. They tolerated the sermon. It was only during the offering that they came to life. As people began to put their gifts for AIDS victims into the offering plates, the cameras started to roll. The television stations did not want to miss capturing the sight of Christians giving to help people who were mostly homosexuals.

The media representatives hung around until the meeting was over. They wanted to interview people in order to get some sense of the reactions of this evangelical audience. As I watched the results of those interviews on the evening news, I really turned on. The results could not have been better.

The first person interviewed was an overweight guy wearing a tee shirt. His stomach was sticking out like some of the old beer drinkers I used to see cheering at wrestling matches. He even had the required tattoo on his arm to give him proper redneck credentials. When asked how he reacted to the offering, the man answered in a semi-belligerent tone, "What are y' talkin' about?"

The TV interviewer went on to say, "The offering was for AIDS victims, and they're usually homosexuals. Do you approve of homosexuality?"

That man's response was beautiful. "I don't know about all that homo stuff," he answered. "All I know is that when people are sick, Christians are supposed to help them!"

What could he have said that would have given better expression to what Christianity is all about? There were none of those pious clichés about "having to hate the sin while loving the sinner" (which is what I would have said). All he gave was a direct statement as to how Christians are supposed to act if they are to be true followers of Christ.

The second interview was with an elderly woman who had all the appearance of an uptight, holier-than-thou paragon of virtue. I thought to myself as the interview began, "Here it comes! They're going to get just the kind of pious condemnation that the world has come to expect from us."

I was wrong! While I could not detect them, I had the feeling that this dear woman's eyes were filling with tears as she spoke. Her voice cracked a bit, and she had to pause twice to regain her composure. "Tonight, for the first time, I feel free to say that my grandson died of AIDS. I have felt that my Christian friends would look down on me and despise my grandson if they knew. Tonight I felt like they care for him." Nothing that I had preached that evening could match the clarity with which she had expressed what the love of Christ is like in the midst of a fallen world.

The expectations of the media people, though unrealized that evening, were justified. The way in which many evangelicals have reacted to the AIDS epidemic has been dishonoring to the name of the church. Some prominent preachers have even declared that AIDS is a special judgment of God upon the homosexual community. And some evangelical authors have put out alarmist books which distort the facts of the situation. Religious demagogues have called for the quarantining of all people with AIDS, even though there is ample evidence that their presence poses almost no health hazard to others unless there is an actual exchange of bodily fluid. Because of such histrionic behavior, those with AIDS have generally picked up the message that the Christian community hates and despises them.

The idea that AIDS is some kind of special condemnation from God upon homosexuals because of their sin not only is absurd; it also dishonors God. All disease and death are allowed by God as consequences of the Fall in the Garden of Eden. But to say that AIDS is a special disease created by God to torture homosexuals suggests that God has a special axe to grind with homosexuals that He does not have with the rest of us.

We are all sinners. And I fail to see why anybody would think that adultery could be less of a sin than homosexual intercourse. I have a hard time believing that turning our backs upon starving children in the pursuit of an affluent lifestyle is a less serious crime in the eyes of God than is the "making out" of homosexual lovers.

It seems to me that if God sent a special disease to hospitalize until death all of us who have done despicable things in His eyes, we would all be lying on hospital beds. Those who claim that homosexuals are somehow more wicked than the rest of us deceive themselves. The sexual infidelity that is wrecking America's marriages and traumatizing millions of children cannot be any better than that which homosexuals might do with each other. Sin is sin. I cannot believe that homosexuals are major league sinners deserving of major league sickness, while the rest of us are entitled to generally good health because we are minor league sinners who are therefore not so bad!

God is not the author of evil:

> Let no man say when he is tempted, I am tempted of God: for God cannot be tempted with evil, neither tempteth he any man (James 1:13).

> For God is not the author of confusion, but of peace, as in all churches of the saints (1 Cor. 14:33).

He weeps over sickness and death, and He sent His Son to conquer both. He wills that the consequences of Adam's Fall be negated:

> For as in Adam all die, even so in Christ shall all be made alive (1 Cor. 15:22).

To make God into a spiteful deity diminishes His goodness in the eyes of many and makes Him into something that He is not.

If anything, AIDS can be seen as the modern-day equivalent of the disease of leprosy as described in the Bible. In New Testament days, people who had leprosy were viewed very much the same way that many modern-day religious people view AIDS victims. Those with leprosy were seen as having their disease because of some special sin they or their fathers had committed. People kept their distance from leprosy victims, believing that even to have the shadows of lepers fall upon them would render them mysteriously contaminated by evil. Certainly, no one would touch a leper. Lepers had to carry a bell when they walked about and constantly ring it while calling out, "Unclean! Unclean!"

All that has been said about lepers can also be said about AIDS victims. They, too, are believed to be spiritually unclean in a way that the rest of us are not. They, too, are "untouchables" who, in some cases, are rejected by even the doctors and nurses who are assigned to care for them. They, like their leper counterparts in the ancient world, are viewed as especially despicable and deserving of being run out of decent society.

Two thousand years ago, when Jesus was physically present among us, He reached out to lepers. He touched the untouchables. He showed special compassion toward those who had been treated in such a cruel manner by the people around them. His willingness to lovingly lay hands on those whom society deemed unclean should set an example for all of us who sing, "I Would Be Like Jesus."

There are some notable examples of Christians who have heeded the challenge which the victims of AIDS have posed for us all. In San Diego, there is a lovely Christian woman who has organized her church friends to start a hospice for those who are dying of AIDS. Realizing that AIDS victims need special love and care which may not readily be available, she has gotten together both the material and the human resources to provide a place where AIDS patients can live out their last days in the context of Christian love. What better way to witness for Christ than to touch the untouchables and to care for those whom the world rejects? What better opportunity to tell the story of God's salvation through Jesus Christ than as good Samaritans?

I believe the AIDS epidemic has provided Christians with a unique opportunity. We have always claimed to "hate the sin and love the sinner"—here is our chance to *show* that we love them. By setting up hospices and serving the thousands who are expected to die as a consequence of this disease, we can demonstrate that we are people who love not only in word, but also in deed—which is what true love always does.

What my friend did for AIDS victims in San Diego should be done by people and churches all over the world. This is our chance to do what few are willing to do, for people whom few are willing to touch. I hope that we will see church people show as much love for AIDS victims as has been shown by actress Elizabeth Taylor, who has worked relentlessly on their behalf. I hope that we will not be outdone in good works for AIDS victims by rock stars giving benefit concerts. I hope that we seize the opportunity of this moment in history to do something splendid for AIDS victims in the name of Christ.

Starting hospices so that AIDS victims can die in an environment of Christian love rather than in the horrible loneliness that is usually their fate in their last days, can be a dramatic sign of Christian concern. AIDS patients report that what they dread most is not dying, but dying alone. Other people are afraid to be with them. Christians, by choosing to minister to AIDS patients, can demonstrate that God equips them with that perfect love which casts out fear:

> There is no fear in love; but perfect love casteth out fear: because fear hath torment. He that feareth is not made perfect in love (1 John 4:18).

Less dramatic but no less important than starting hospices is being communicators of the truth about AIDS. Dr. C. Everett Koop, Surgeon General of the United States, under the Reagan administration, is an evangelical brother of very deep commitment, and his word can be trusted. Through a pamphlet distributed to every home in America, he has been trying to get us to understand that the following things are true:

> AIDS is primarily communicated through both homosexual and heterosexual intercourse. Casual contact or interaction with AIDS victims will not provide the conditions necessary to get the disease. The AIDS virus must be put into the blood stream directly for the disease to be transmitted. Touching AIDS victims is safe. There is no need to quarantine AIDS victims or to treat them in an antisocial manner in order to maintain public safety.

In some places, the fear of AIDS victims has created almost panic conditions. Stories about hemophiliac children who have gotten AIDS from blood transfusions being driven out of public schools are becoming common. Demands by workers in some factories and offices that persons with AIDS be fired are more and more frequent. Christians must struggle against such hysteria.

A Baptist church in San Francisco recently made a courageous statement about the AIDS issue. The leaders of the church's day school were approached by parents who wanted to know if their child, who was infected with the AIDS virus, might be accepted as a student. There was a strong possibility that the parents of other children in the school might react negatively and not only pull their children out of the school but also take their memberships out of the church.

The good news is that the church leaders did the right thing and welcomed the infected child into the school. In so doing, they made a strong statement about their views on the AIDS issue, taking a stand against the fears that too often are propagated in evangelical circles. I wish that more churches would be this bold for the cause of justice. Wouldn't it be wonderful if Christian day schools stood ready to accept children infected with AIDS when community people demand that they be expelled from the public school system? This would provide great justification for the creation of Christian schools!

It is not uncommon to hear our evangelical leaders preaching that we should love people who are homosexuals and endeavor to lead them to Christ. What evangelicals do in response to the AIDS epidemic will largely determine how well we can carry out such a mandate. If we show love by accepting and caring for those infected with the AIDS virus, we will have taken a positive step toward earning the right to be heard by our homosexual brothers and sisters. If we fail to do what is right in this crisis, we will be making a statement that our words can never overcome.

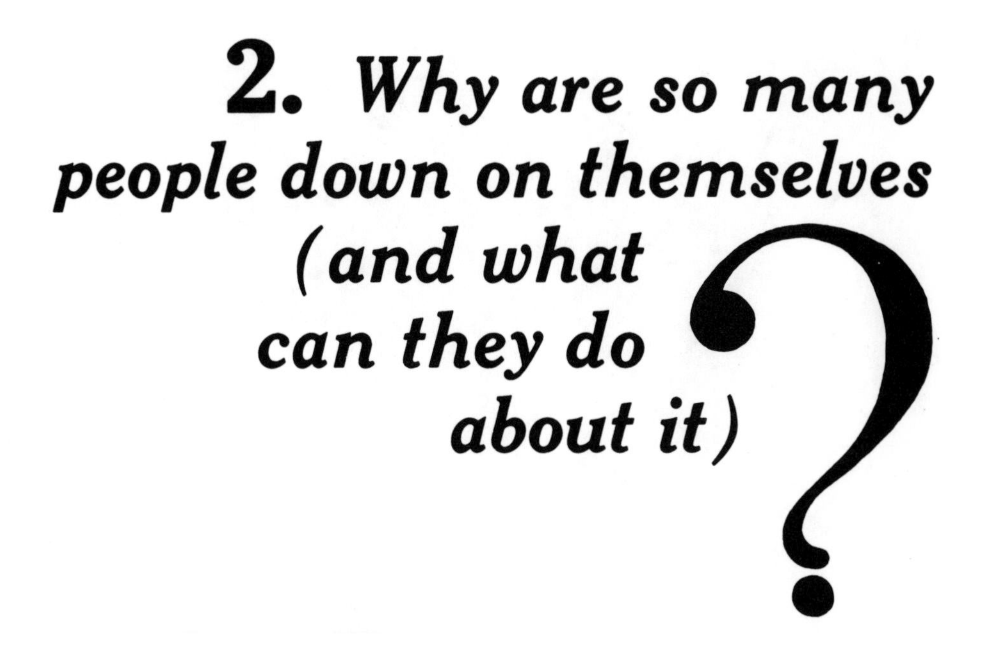
2. Why are so many
people down on themselves
(and what
can they do
about it)
?

A FRIEND OF MINE has an adorable four-year-old daughter. She is bright, and she is talkative. If tryouts were being held for a modern-day Shirley Temple, I think she would win, hands down.

One night there was a violent thunderstorm. The lightning flashed and the thunder rumbled—it was one of those terrifying storms that forces everyone to stop and tremble a bit. My friend ran upstairs to his daughter's bedroom to see if she were frightened and to assure her that everything would be all right. He got to her room and found her standing on the window sill, spread-eagled against the glass. When he shouted, "What are you doing?", she turned away from the flashing lightning and happily reported, "I think that God is trying to take my picture."

Why don't most people feel that important—that good about themselves? Why don't most people like themselves as much as that little girl likes herself? Why are so many people down on themselves, and why do some even hate themselves?

I find that there is not too much correlation between people's circumstances and accomplishments and their self-concepts. I know people who definitely are socially successful, having achieved a significant number of worthwhile things in their lives, and who despise themselves. Contrariwise, I know others who by societal standards have not accomplished much at all, but who think of themselves as worthwhile and valuable.

Having a positive self-concept is of great importance not only for our own sense of well-being but for the well-being of all of those whom we meet in our everyday activities. I have found that people who like themselves are people who like everyone else they meet, and that those who are down on themselves are down on everyone else.

Check out this thesis in your own experience: Is it not true that the people you know who are always saying positive things about those with whom they live and work are the ones who basically feel good about themselves? And is it not also true in your experience that those who are nasty to others are themselves filled with self-contempt?

Part of what makes us feel bad about ourselves can be traced back to the ways we think we are viewed by the people around us, particularly those people who play the most important roles in our lives. Your husband or your wife, for instance, can make you feel wonderful about yourself but he or she is also capable of cutting your sense of self-worth down to nothing. Parents and close friends can do this, too. I have often watched people destroy the self-esteem of a loved one right before my eyes.

A few months ago, I was a guest speaker for a citywide evangelistic service. Thousands of people were present, and there was a euphoric quality to the gathering. The excitement of the crowd and the presence of the Holy Spirit made the evening a memorable and blessed time.

When the service was over, a middle-aged couple pulled me aside to talk. Or perhaps I should say that the *wife* got me aside to talk—because she was the one who did all the talking. She gushed all over me and told me how wonderful I was, and she remarked that it must be very exciting for my wife to be married to me. All of that flattery made me a bit uneasy. But what really upset me was her not-too-subtle implication that the man to whom she was married was, by comparison, rather boring. I felt that, while flattering me, she was simultaneously putting down her husband. By the end of her effusive praise, I wondered not only how her husband felt about me, but also how he felt about himself.

Of course, there are also many ways in which men put down their wives. One of the most evil side effects of soft porn magazines like *Playboy* is that the wives of those men who are "into" centerfolds are often made to feel inferior by comparison. It is easy for them to begin to feel that their husbands find them relatively unattractive. Middle-aged women are especially prone to a sense of self-contempt about their physical appearance because our culture defines beauty in very sexist and youth-oriented ways.

I do a bit of consulting work with my good friend Wayne Alderson's Value of the Person, a labor/management team that helps industries apply Christian principles to the activities of the workplace. Wayne has let me know that the complaint most often voiced by workers is over put-downs that come from bosses. He contends that most employers seem afraid to give affirmation and to make workers feel special and important. From his observations, it seems as though most employers try to convey to their workers that because they are easily replaceable, they had better be careful and do what they are told.

Wayne contends that because workers are often made to feel that they are valueless, they usually want union leaders who are tough and demanding with management. Without a personal sense of being valuable, workers can equate their worth only by how much money they can earn and how much security they can write into contracts.

According to Wayne, such feelings are the reason most relationships between workers and management go sour. Workers who have been regularly put down by their employers use union negotiations as opportunities to send a message to management that they are men and women and not simply things to be pushed around like machines. They are using the only means available to them to say that they are persons who are worth something.

At Value of the Person labor/management seminars, management and union members are brought together to express their feelings about themselves and each other. I will never forget attending one of these get-togethers at which a huge steelworker broke down and cried. The sight of this hulk of a man staring at the floor, his body trembling, brushing tears away from his cheeks is etched indelibly on my mind. I can still hear him saying, "You guys in management make me feel like s______!" While four-letter words are not as likely to be used by those of us proper types who go to offices each day, many of us can identify with that steelworker's feelings, because we feel exactly the same way in our own jobs.

Whatever others may do to us and to our self-images, many of us are filled with self-contempt because of what we do to ourselves. We do not have to experience put-downs from others to feel bad about ourselves; most of us can do a pretty good job of self-deprecation without any outside assistance.

Sometimes we even put ourselves down for religious reasons. There are times when our religion makes us too introspective for our own good. Spending more time than we should trying to discover all the sins in our lives can guarantee that we will end up depressed. If we concentrate too much on rooting out the evil that lies within us, we will find much more than we can handle.

I am not suggesting that we should ignore our sin, but I do believe that we should come to enjoy the grace of God. When Jesus died on the cross, He took *all* of our sin upon Himself—even those sins which we may have forgotten. According to the gospel, Jesus experienced on the cross all the condemnation necessary for what we have been and what we have done. Instead of condemning ourselves, therefore, we should bask in the good news that "there is therefore now no condemnation to them which are in Christ Jesus" (Rom. 8:1). If Christ has delivered us from condemnation, then we have no right to be down on ourselves. Having cast our sins upon Jesus, we ought to leave them behind and begin to press on to see ourselves in a positive light (Phil. 3:13–14).

Sigmund Freud once made the statement that the church is in the business of delivering people from guilt, but that if people do not *feel* guilt, then the church makes it its duty to *create* guilt. That way, the church can deliver people from what it has made them feel. Unfortunately, the church usually does a much better job of creating guilt than it does in providing deliverance from it.

I think that Freud was partly right. Too often we have allowed ourselves to be subject to a brand of Christianity that makes more of our sinfulness than it does of God's grace. We must know that "where sin abounded, grace did much more abound" (Rom. 5:20).

A lot of people criticize the popular television preacher Robert Schuller, claiming that he does not adequately point out that we are sinners. The truth is that Schuller *does* point out sin for his listeners, but he puts more of an emphasis on the grace of God. Schuller is able to help people feel good about themselves by convincing them that in Christ, they are not condemned for their sinfulness, but loved for their wonderful possibilities.

A prominent preacher in the Philadelphia area became involved with another man's wife. A divorce resulted, and the preacher lost his pulpit. As he picked up the pieces of his life and tried to put them back together again, I met with him occasionally to see how he was doing and try to be of some help. One day I asked him if he had found himself a new church home where he could worship and grow. He told me that he did not go to church anymore, but that he did listen regularly to Robert Schuller. I was surprised at his response, but he went on to say, "When a person has been through what I have been through, he doesn't need to be told that he's a sinner. He needs to hear that by the grace of God he has great possibilities, and that is what Schuller tells me."

I do not want to go on and on about Schuller here. But I do believe he has latched on to a powerful psychological and spiritual truth: Too much negative introspection in an effort to achieve some kind of spiritual perfection can do a terrible job on us! We need to remind ourselves, as Scripture reminds us, that God's grace has given us wonderful possibilities:

> But as many as received him, to them gave he power to become the sons of God, even to them that believe on his name (John 1:12).

> Beloved, now are we the sons of God, and it doth not yet appear what we shall be: but we know that, when he shall appear, we shall be like him; for we shall see him as he is (1 John 3:2).

Another way in which we often do a negative job on ourselves is by failing to take care of ourselves physically. There is a close connection between our physical well-being and our spiritual and psychological well-being. If we allow ourselves to get overtired or rundown, chances are we will end up depressed and maybe even hating ourselves.

I tend to be prone to this kind of self-induced physical abuse. Sometimes I overextend myself, work too hard or try to accomplish too much, and end up physically exhausted. What is worse, in order to keep myself going, I sometimes drink several cups of coffee a day and eat candy bars to get quick bursts of energy. Naturally, all of this sets me up for depression. I am left not only feeling physically down, but also telling myself what a lousy person I am. My dilapidated condition not only makes me hard on myself; it makes me hard on everybody else around me. Self-contempt always leads to contempt for others.

If you find that you are really down on yourself, take some time off, rest up, check your diet, and make sure that the cause of how you feel is not self-inflicted physical abuse. Make sure that your body, which is "the temple of God," is treated with loving respect. You and everybody around you will suffer if you don't.

Self-contempt also can come from wasting time. Have you ever had a day off and wasted it on something as meaningless as watching hours of television or just sitting around doing nothing? Do you recall how you felt at the end of the day?—probably depressed and a bit down on yourself! If you repeated that kind of thing for several days in a row, you might really end up with a good dose of self-contempt. Wasting time may be one of the most devastating consequences of being on welfare. If you just sit around being lazy week after week because you have nothing of worth to do with your time, you will probably end up hating yourself—and others.

Activities which can alleviate a sense of wasting time are manifold. The easiest thing to do is to learn something. A day spent adding to your storehouse of knowledge is a day that will end up giving you a sense of accomplishment and well-being. To learn something new and important is to guarantee that you will feel good about yourself. For example, many retired people have been able to overcome the sense of worthlessness that sometimes accompanies inactivity by going back to college or taking classes at a community center.

In the Hebraic tradition, learning the Torah was considered to be an end in itself, and those who were able to spend their time learning the things of God thought themselves to be very fortunate. There is much about that ancient Hebraic tradition which is applicable to our own lives. If you are down on yourself and you have the time, go back to school and learn about the things of God. Perhaps there is a Bible college or seminary nearby that has an adult education program. If not, try the community college in your area and take some religion or philosophy courses there. Learning about God is great therapy for those who have the need to improve the way they feel about themselves. So is learning about all that is in the world He has given us. As T. H. White wrote in *The Once and Future King,*

> The best thing for being sad . . . is to learn something. That is the only thing that never fails. You may grow old and trembling in your anatomies, you may lie awake at night listening to the disorder of your veins, you may miss your only love, you may see the world about you devastated by evil lunatics, or know your honour trampled in the sewers of baser minds. There is only one thing for it then—to learn. Learn why the world wags and what wags it.[1]

Doing good and serving others are other ways out of the doldrums of self-contempt. The missionary organization which I

1. Terence H. White, *The Once and Future King* (New York: G. P. Putnam's Sons/Berkley Medallion Books, 1966), p. 183.

helped to establish, the Evangelical Association for the Promotion of Education, has an outreach program among urban children who are having problems with their schoolwork. In order to help these children, our organization enlists people to tutor them and to help them with their homework.

As we did our initial recruiting, we were able to find a half-dozen very well educated women who were free and willing to help us in our efforts. Two of them were in psychotherapy because their negative feelings about themselves were so severe. But these two women were in for a surprising transformation. As they helped troubled inner-city children, they themselves found help. In serving the children, they began to sense their own worth. Doing something important for others made them feel that *they* were important. One of the women who had been in psychotherapy acknowledged that working with the kids had done more good for her than had her therapist. It was what she had done for others that was her psychological salvation. I am sure that Jesus had this in mind when He said,

> For whosoever will save his life shall lose it: and whosoever will lose his life for my sake shall find it. For what is a man profited, if he shall gain the whole world, and lose his own soul? or what shall a man give in exchange for his soul? (Matt. 16:25–26).

I can never understand why people who are down on themselves do not grasp how easy it is to redefine their worth through meaningful service to others. There are always lonely people to be visited, visitation evangelism to be done, and children who need loving attention. I know that if those who are depressed would forget themselves (as Jesus suggests) and lose themselves in other people who need them, they would realize a great sense of self-worth.

There are a host of opportunities for short-term missionary work with periods of service that run from as short as two weeks to as long as two years. There are openings in various countries around the world as well as within the United States. My own missionary organization serves as a clearinghouse for persons who are looking for places where they can make long-lasting and important contributions for Christ and His kingdom. If you do not know where to turn for short-term missionary assignments, just write to me at:

The Evangelical Association for the Promotion of Education (EAPE)
Box 238
St. Davids, Pennsylvania 19087

People on my staff will be more than happy to help you to find a place where you can do for others the things that will insure your own sense of positive self-worth.

One final thing that can help if you are down on yourself is to try to recover the dreams of your childhood. Think back to when you had a vision for doing something wonderful with your life. All of us have unrealized dreams. Each of us can think of something glorious we "should have done" with our lives. Reconsider the options abandoned. Take another look at what might have been. Perhaps one of the reasons you are down on yourself is that you are angry with yourself for not stepping out and taking a good shot at fulfilling your own hopes for life. The dream that was once your own may have been given to you by God.

So often people tell me that they hate themselves because they have failed to become what they once hoped to be. Those who say such things reproach themselves most because they have never even tried. My advice to all such reluctant dreamers is "Go for it!" It is never too late. One of the advantages of the long life expectancy most Americans enjoy today is that it is possible to attempt several vocations before our lives are ended. Having earned the money to put the kids through school, why not spend the rest of your life living out the impossible dream that you have secretly entertained for years?

I was preaching at a church one evening and really hitting on this theme. I told about Abraham who, "when his life was far spent," made the decision to live out the vision that God had given him. I pointed out that the entire eleventh chapter of Hebrews is nothing more than a listing of men and women who risked everything, including looking foolish, in order to respond to the dreams which God had placed in their hearts and minds. Faith, I declared, is nothing more and nothing less than believing that with God all things are possible—even careers of service when others are expecting you to retire.

When I was finished speaking, I felt that God had touched some hearts. This feeling was confirmed when a middle-aged couple came up to talk to me about their lives. That conversation led them to make some important decisions. And today that couple is part of a missionary team working in Paterson, New Jersey. They are helping some of the most disadvantaged children in America to find Christ and to have better lives. There is no doubt in my mind that this husband and wife feel terrific about themselves.

If your self-esteem is lagging, why don't you try something daring? If you do not take risks in living, you may risk not living at all. Once, when they asked Helen Keller if there was anything she could think of that was worse than being blind, she answered, "Yes! Being able to see and having no vision."

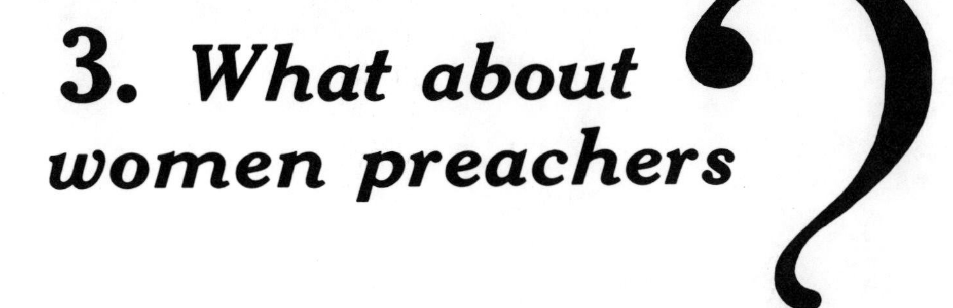
3. What about
women preachers
?

A FEW YEARS AGO I was asked to be the speaker for a Bible conference. The other person who was to share the speaking responsibilities for the week was a very bright, articulate woman who happens to be a good friend of mine. I looked forward to the conference, knowing that our families would have a pleasant time together. Neither of us was prepared for the barrage of criticism that came from Christian people who felt that having a woman as a preacher was unbiblical.

Recently, I was a speaker for a large assembly of Seventh Day Adventists. Some evangelicals believe that these brothers and sisters are part of a cult that negates the essence of the gospel. However, ever since the stalwart Donald Grey Barnhouse, one of the deans of evangelical theology, carefully examined their theology and ended up by declaring them fellow Christians, most of us have regarded the Adventists as very much a part of the Protestant mainstream.

Consequently, I was sure that I would find much with which to agree in the teachings of the Adventist church—and I did. I appreciated their emphasis on observing the Sabbath, even though I felt that they made too big a deal out of its having to be on Saturday:

> One man esteemeth one day above another: another esteemeth every day alike. Let every man be fully persuaded in his own mind. He that regardeth the day, regardeth it unto the Lord; and he that regardeth not the day, to the Lord he doth not regard it. He that eateth, eateth to the Lord, for he giveth God thanks; and he that eateth not, to the Lord he eateth not, and giveth God thanks (Rom. 14:5–6).

I thought their dietary habits made a lot of sense. The emphasis they placed on salvation through Christ was in harmony with my own beliefs.

What surprised me was the Adventist rejection of the idea of ordaining women as ministers. The reason that their views on this subject seemed so strange to me is that their denomination was founded by a woman. Ellen White was the one whose prophecies gave form to the Seventh Day Adventist movement. Her teachings have served as the official creedal position of Adventist churches, and there is general acknowledgment that Ellen White was a spokesperson for God to whom all Adventists must give attention. How a Protestant denomination which was founded by a woman preacher can refuse to ordain women to the gospel ministry is beyond me!

As a child growing up in an evangelical church, I was regularly exposed to missionaries. Our pastor was committed to the missionary movement and, in an effort to encourage a consciousness of the need to proclaim the gospel to the billion people outside the Christian faith, he invited missionaries to occupy his pulpit several times each year. Many of these missionary speakers were women. These women told about their work in Africa, Latin America, and Asia. They told about their preaching and their work in planting churches. They usually were exciting preachers whose zeal and gifts gave ample evidence that they had been called by God to do their special work.

Consequently, I was confused when I learned that my church did not approve of the ordination of women. It seemed to me that there was a contradiction in giving women authority to preach to people in other countries and then denying them the privilege of being ordained for ministry in our country.

In my opinion, evangelical Christianity in general has evidenced a hypocritical duplicity by sending women to be preachers in difficult situations overseas while denying them the right to be ministers in the United States. And I suspect that one of the reasons women have been kept out of our pulpits is economic. Undoubtedly, if women were readily admitted to the ordained ministry of the church, they would provide competition for pulpits that have already become scarce for clergymen who want them.

Also, there are those fears that men have about women, which feminist psychologists and sociologists such as Mary Daly have made all too clear. For instance, some men feel that if they are under the leadership of women they will lose status in the eyes of other men. Then there are men who feel their sexual potency will be threatened if women are put above them in any kind of hierarchical system. In the eyes of such men, male sexuality is always built on dominance.

But too often these real reasons for opposing the ordination of women are hidden by theological rationalizations generated by religious male chauvinists—and even by some women who find a variety of benefits for themselves in the traditional position which the church has prescribed for women.

Some people sincerely do believe that Scripture prohibits the ordination of women. They usually cite certain Scripture references to make their case. Most often quoted is:

> Let the woman learn in silence with all subjection. But I suffer not a woman to teach, nor to usurp authority over the man, but to be in silence (1 Tim. 2:11–12).

Upon first reading, this verse clearly seems to say that women ought not to say anything at church meetings, let alone be ordained as ministers. However, those church leaders who use this text to beat down evangelical feminists are not about to fire all the female Sunday school teachers, youth directors, and Christian Education directors from the staffs of their churches. They are well aware of the fact that without women, the programs of their churches would fall apart.

Usually these church leaders do a bit of unconvincing double talk as they endeavor to make a fine differentiation between teaching and preaching. They try to say that it is okay for women to teach but not to preach. Of course, when it comes to Sunday school teachers, they ignore the fact that the apostle Paul apparently does not recognize this distinction—he categorically says that women should say nothing in church—period!

This passage in Timothy once posed a very serious problem for me because I am one of those who believes in the infallibility of the Scriptures. It was inconceivable to me that Paul could have made a mistake when he wrote these words because I am convinced that the Holy Spirit guided Paul and kept him from errors. However, recent biblical scholarship has shown me that my former reading of this passage was limited by a failure to understand what was going on in the church of the first century. Lately I have come to read this passage with a whole new interpretation.

It seems as though the women in the early church were abusing their new-found Christian freedom. The realization that in Christ there was "neither male nor female" (Gal. 3:28) and that women stood before God as equals to men led them to be carried away into excesses which were both shocking and unkind. Many evangelical scholars contend that these women, emancipated by their new status in Christ, were standing up in church meetings and putting down their husbands, giving them lectures on how they should behave. The humiliation of husbands whose shortcomings were being publicly exposed apparently had become scandalous. These scholars believe that Paul was trying to put an end to this embarrassing behavior when he wrote,

> And if they will learn any thing, let them ask their husbands at home: for it is a shame for women to speak in the church (1 Cor. 14:35).

He was simply declaring that domestic problems should be dealt with in private and that women should not abuse the privileges they had found through Christ's liberation by behaving in an unseemly fashion. Church was not the place for them to try to teach their husbands what those husbands should and should not do.

While I may not agree with those people in Christian traditions which exclude women from *all* leadership roles in which they might exercise teaching or preaching authority over men, I do respect their consistency. What I find hard to accept are those who readily allow women to be missionaries and preach to men overseas or allow them to be Sunday school teachers here at home, yet still contend that women should be silent in church!

During the nineteenth century, a significant proportion of the Baptist churches in Maine and in Wisconsin were pastored by women because no men were willing to take the positions. Yet today many of those same churches condemn women preachers and pretend that they are part of a religious tradition that never accepted them.

Whether or not one accepts these perspectives on Pauline scripture, there are still other grounds being provided by biblical scholars which will give further warrant to abandoning traditional prohibitions against women preachers. Recently, in personal conversations with theologians from two of the nation's most theologically conservative seminaries, I learned that there was good reason to believe Paul never intended that women be forever excluded from exercising leadership in church. These two theologians contend that Paul meant the prohibition of women preachers only in times and places where women leaders would be scandalous to those in the society outside the church.

The argument of these scholars is that if the existence of women preachers created a barrier to non-Christians' coming into the faith, then it was right for women to refrain from being preachers. In today's world, they point out, keeping women *out* of pulpits is having a negative effect upon the propagation of the gospel throughout the outside world, and therefore the policy on the matter which was in place in the past should be set aside.

What was most sad about my conversations with these theologians was that they were afraid to lend support to this point of view by allowing their names or their schools to be mentioned publicly. They told me that if they were identified, their schools would lose many students and much of their financial support. However, both of these men felt that integrity would not allow them to remain silent much longer. They told me that during the next two or three years they will have completed the research to fully justify their case and will then challenge their seminaries and their students to change their positions on the ordination of women.

The changed status of women through the work of Christ was graphically dramatized in what happened the day Christ was crucified. As you may recall, the temple on Mount Zion was divided into three major sections. The first was the Holy of Holies, which contained the Ark of the Covenant, on which was located the mercy seat (Exod. 26:31–37). Once a year, on the Day of Atonement, the designated high priest of the temple entered the Holy of Holies and poured onto the mercy seat the blood of a lamb, thus symbolizing that there would some day be a savior, the ultimate Lamb of God, whose shed blood would cover the sins of all people once and for all (Heb. 10:10–12).

Second, there was the Holy Place. This was a section of the temple reserved for Jewish men who, in the Hebraic tradition, were the first-class citizens of God's kingdom. Finally, there was the Outer Court. This was the place in the temple where women and Gentiles could worship. There was no doubt that in the ancient Jewish world, women and Gentiles were "far off" (that is, in a place of inferiority), and denied the privileged status which Jewish men had before the Lord.

When Jesus was crucified, the stratification system expressed in the construction of the temple was changed in an awesome fashion. The Bible tells us that upon the death of Christ there was an earthquake, and the wall that separated the Jewish men from the women and Gentiles was ripped down (Luke 23:44–46). The apostle Paul saw great significance in this event. For Paul, the destruction of the dividing wall that separated Jewish men from others was evidence that the hierarchical system of the Old Testament had been abolished. He writes,

> For he is our peace, who hath made both one, and hath broken down the middle wall of partition between us; Having abolished in his flesh the enmity, even the law of commandments contained in ordinances; for to make in himself of twain one new man, so making peace; And that he might reconcile both unto God in one body by the cross, having slain the enmity thereby (Eph. 2:14–16).

The meaning of this is clear. Thus he writes, "For ye are all the children of God by faith in Christ Jesus" (Gal. 3:26).

In Christ, the inferiority of Gentiles and women was abolished. All the privileges which hitherto were enjoyed only by men were now theirs. The work of the Holy Spirit was no longer limited by secular differentiations; He now imparted his gifts to females as well as to males. This is the message Peter declared on the day of Pentecost:

> And it shall come to pass in the last days, saith God, I will pour out of my Spirit upon all flesh: and your sons and your daughters shall prophesy, and your young men shall see visions, and your old men shall dream dreams: And on my servants and on my handmaidens I will pour out in those days of my Spirit; and they shall prophesy (Acts 2:17–18).

When Peter said that people would receive gifts, he in no way suggested that only men would be recipients of these gifts. In fact, he made it clear that women also would receive them. And he went on to let us know in no uncertain terms that those who have such gifts of the Spirit ought to use them in Christian service.

In light of this giving of spiritual gifts to *both* men and women, it is no surprise that on the day of Pentecost, Peter shared the good news that *both* men and women would declare God's message to the world. (In this passage of Acts, the word here translated as "prophesy" means "to preach.") Nor is it any surprise that when the first deacons were appointed to lead the Macedonian church, a woman named Cleo was named to the office, nor that Paul acknowledged Euodias and Syntyche, two women, as leaders and cofounders of the church at Philippi.

In Christ, a new day had dawned, and the old power structures which had made some persons less viable than others as instruments of God were gone. In Christ, women and Gentiles were lifted up to positions once held only by Jewish men.

I thank God for this New Testament message. Without it, we would have missed out on the ministries of many wonderful women who have given incredibly important leadership to the church. Christendom has been blessed with the likes of Katherine Kuhlman, the American preacher and healer. The poor of America have received the tender mercies of those wonderful uniformed women of the Salvation Army who so faithfully have declared the message of salvation as they cheerfully lived out Christian charity. The history of the church would have been diminished without such luminaries as Antoinette L. Brown, America's first fully ordained woman; Phoebe Palmer, the feminist writer who penned *Promise of the Father;* and, Christable Pankhurst, the Christian leader of the British suffrage movement who preached God's word with faithfulness.

Recently I spent some time with a Roman Catholic bishop who explained to me how women had been a godsend to many of the churches in his diocese which lacked priestly leadership. He explained that nuns were serving as the pastors for many of his rural congregations, although the people did not actually call them pastors. These nuns visited the sick, taught the catechism, preached the homilies, and even served Holy Communion. He explained that once a month, he or one of his auxiliary bishops would visit each of these female-led parishes, perform the mass, and sanctify the bread and wine. These "sanctified elements" would then be stored until worship time, when they would be given to communicants by the nuns. When I pointed out that these nuns did everything that priests do and therefore should be ordained, he agreed. Then he added, "Most people in these parishes would also agree, but you know how the church is." Indeed I do!

Throughout the rest of American Christendom, women are becoming more and more evident in church leadership. I think that some of us are just catching on to the implications of the ways in which Christ changed the status of women. We have begun to allow them to have the pulpits of small congregations when no viable male member of the clergy is available. Christendom is still keeping women from its most prestigious pulpits, but it won't be long before we will all be forced to grow up and grasp the message about women that God has been trying to declare to us for the last two thousand years.

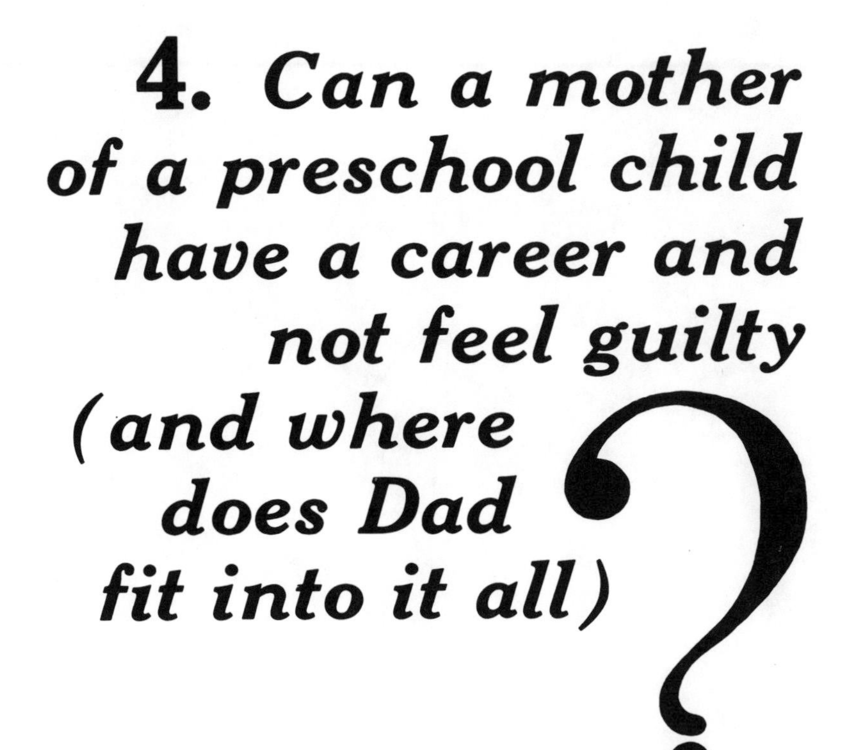
4. Can a mother
of a preschool child
have a career and
not feel guilty
(and where
does Dad
fit into it all)
?

I KNOW THAT as a supporter of Christian feminism I am supposed to say "Yes!" without reservation to the question of careers for mothers of preschoolers. But to be perfectly honest, I must say that I *do* have reservations.

I think it is time for those of us who advocate the feminist value system to take a second look at what is happening to children in America and ask if mothers *and fathers* should not be doing much better by them. It is time to face the fact that in most cases being a good mother (like being a good father) requires significant sacrifices in career development.

The problems posed for a career by having children are difficult for both sexes, but they are particularly severe for women. There are cultural expectations that women be the primary agents for raising children. From time immemorial, role expectations for women have included being the primary persons involved in the socialization of children.

Of course, there are some who will read the above statements and properly exclaim, "That's what's wrong with society! Why should the woman be expected to be the "love machine"? Why is it the mother who is always required to meet the emotional needs of children? Why can't the father, at least in part, take over this role?"

And they have a point—up to a point! Men *have* been negligent in providing emotional support in the raising of children. There is a general acknowledgment that the macho man of the past, who brushed off his obligation to care for his children with a simple declaration that it was "women's work," made a serious mistake.

Personally, I have often wished that when our children were babies I had been more involved in caring for them. Being a father in less enlightened days delivered me from the unpleasantness of changing many dirty diapers, but it also denied me much of the emotional gratification which might have been mine if I had been more involved in meeting my children's affectional needs. Now I am envious when I see "liberated" young fathers enjoying taking care of their babies in ways that were uncommon thirty years ago.

New models for family life are offering options to men who want to be significantly involved in rearing their children. I know a young husband who is getting a real kick out of sharing child-rearing responsibilities with his wife. She has a job that requires a good bit of travel, and during her times away he assumes almost total responsibility for the care of their two children. He is a commercial artist, and much of his work can be done at home. His studio hours are flexible and allow him to be on hand when he is needed.

This young husband is quite delighted to meet his children when they return home from school. He is ever ready to make time to attend special events at school. He is available to take his children to the dentist and to provide the kind of taxi service that is often a requisite for children in suburbia. When the children were in their preschool years, he shared the work of caring for them on a fifty-fifty basis with his wife. By being equal partners in the responsibilities that go with raising their children, they have been providing constant parental love and support day in and day out. Their children know that there will always be a parent present when needed.

But this is an atypical family. Not too many fathers have the kinds of jobs that allow them to call their own shots when it comes to prescribing working hours. Most husbands are caught in the kind of employment that requires that they go to work at nine and quit at five (unless they're "lucky" enough to become executives—then they go to work at eight and get home at seven).

Most women who opt for careers are caught in the same bind. Whether they work as secretaries or as executives, they usually find that their work schedules lack the kind of flexibility that allows for quality time with their children when they want or need it.

Often two-career families must face the unpleasant reality that *neither* of them will be home when the kids return from school. When children are under the age of five, two-career families often assume that they have no alternative but to hold onto their jobs and to put their infants into some form of day care.

Many American women face even more painful circumstances—they must raise their children all by themselves. The single-parent family headed by a female is an increasingly common occurrence in our modern world, and the single mother is forced to earn money to support herself and her children. When there is a divorce, and there are many of them, the standard of living for the single father can be expected to go up, while that of the single mother is usually abruptly and markedly diminished. Like it or not, most single mothers have to get jobs outside the home.

Even people who believe that there is a strong religious argument for women to be full-time mothers are willing, with regret, to accept the fact that there are many women who have no choice but to work outside the home. They shake their heads and declare that mothers' leaving their little children in the hands of others is one of the tragic consequences of divorce, separation, desertion, and widowhood. But these ardent traditionalists have trouble understanding those mothers who *want* to work at outside jobs, whether or not they have to. They cannot grasp the proposition that some mothers believe careers outside the home provide them with emotional gratification and personal identities that are essential for their personal happiness.

Such traditionalists must face the fact that mothering children cannot be what it once was. Motherhood has become extremely difficult and often ungratifying in our modern, transient, urban, industrial society. In previous times mothers were not so much on their own as they often are today. Mothers in bygone days raised their children with the help, not only of husbands who worked at home on the farm, but also with the support of their extended families. Young mothers often had as neighbors their own mothers, who were available to help and advise them. Often there were aunts and sisters close by to provide relief when the burden of child care grew heavy and a few hours of relief were needed.

In today's society, mothers are not so fortunate. Fathers seldom work at home, and marriage usually removes young families from close proximity to their relatives. Often a newly married couple must locate in an apartment building in a city far removed from the extended family. When children are born, the young mother is on her own to figure out what to do with her baby. And there is no relief from the endless hours of child care required of her. For the better part of every day, she has only her child-care book to tell her what to do when her baby is sick or upset. The often solitary woman, trying to chase after one active child all day long while keeping dry diapers on another, can easily find the role of motherhood too much of a drain—a role from which she longs for relief, if not escape.

Making matters worse for the modern mother is that there has been very little, if anything, in her educational experiences to prepare her for the role of primary agent for the care of her preschool child. All the way through elementary and secondary school, she took the same courses as the boys did, with the possible exception of a course or two in home economics (which are becoming increasingly rare in American schools). If she went to college, this mother probably had her intellectual appetite whetted for reading good novels, enjoying the arts, and functioning in a professional environment. Quite simply, almost everything she learned encouraged her toward a career outside the home.

The emergence of babysitters as a prominent American institution is evidence of just how desperate young mothers can get in their effort to escape from constant child care even for a few hours. Having babysitters is a relatively new phenomenon. In days gone by, mothers had all kinds of relatives—sisters, aunts, and grandmothers—readily available to take over and give them relief time. It is a measure of the desperation of the isolated modern mother that some of them will give over the care of precious children to an untrained, inexperienced teenager.

I teach at a small Christian liberal arts college located in the midst of an upper-middle-class suburb. Many of the students have a difficult time coming up with the money needed to finance their educations. Among the employment opportunities close at hand, the most available is babysitting. Almost nightly there are phone calls to our dormitories for students to "sit" with the children of neighboring families. Available students are readily hired, even though the parents who make the calls know almost nothing about the background of the persons they are hiring.

I am not suggesting that we eliminate babysitters. They are an essential part of modern life. However, I do believe that churches can address the need for babysitters in a systematic and caring manner. There are many reliable persons in most churches who could be free to babysit for young couples if they were contacted and scheduled to do so. As a matter of fact, I can think of few ways that older couples in churches could more graciously serve the kingdom and bless young parents than to be available as free babysitters once a week for those who need this help and would be hard-pressed to pay for it.

If I were a pastor, I would try to set up such a babysitting service for the young married couples of my church, and I would call on older couples to recognize their responsibility to help strengthen the marriages of young parents by giving them regular nights off to date. I would even hold training sessions for these volunteers so that they might know how to maximize their ministries both to the children and to the parents involved.

Not only would such a plan provide real blessings for young families; it could be a source of great joy to older couples whose own grandchildren are growing up hundreds of miles away. And I am sure that when word of our church babysitting service got out, a host of new young couples would join, convinced that here was a church that really cared about them.

But even though it is understandable that the pressures of full-time child care in an isolated, unsupported environment are enough to make women *want* to choose outside employment, we also need to look honestly at the possible negative effects such outside employment may have on the children.

For instance, in a recent study of middle-class children conducted by Deborah Lowe Vandell and Mary Anne Corasaniti of the University of Texas, it was discovered that children who are in day care during preschool years are more likely, by the time they reach the third grade, to be uncooperative and unpopular than those in a control group composed of children raised by full-time mothers. These researchers discovered that children who had been in full-time child-care programs during preschool years demonstrated poorer study skills, lower grades, and diminished self-esteem in later years. Vandell and Corasaniti suggest that extensive child care during a child's first year is significantly correlated with retarded social, emotional, and intellectual development.

On a more positive note for mothers who work outside the home, the study also showed that mothers with *part-time* jobs who put their children into day care for less than thirty hours a week had relatively well-adjusted, well-developed children. Perhaps the lesson to be learned from this study is that women who have a choice in the matter should opt for part-time employment, especially during their children's preschool years.

Unfortunately, part-time work with good pay is hard to come by. Employers are well aware that women who are desperate to work part time in order to be more available for their children are easy to exploit, and they quite frequently take advantage of these women. For the most part, those who take part-time jobs have no way to protest their poor pay. It is unlikely that they belong to any union or have any bargaining power. Employers seem to have a readily available pool of replacements for any part-timers who register their discontent.

Christian institutions are not exempt from this tendency to exploit. Churches often take advantage of those seeking part-time work by hiring secretaries and custodians at substandard wages. I find that my own college, like many others which are deeply committed to the evangelical tradition, makes a common practice of hiring part-time teachers at a pittance. The administrators of my college readily admit that underpaying part-time teachers is an essential part of their ability to operate the college on a balanced budget.

If Christians are supposed to be people who speak out for the oppressed, then it may be time to let our voices be heard and our political clout felt by those who perpetrate unfair pay for part-time workers. To those who have become intrigued with the implications of the liberation theologies of Latin America, perhaps it is time to work for the liberation of the oppressed in our own work force—particularly if the oppressed are underpaid mothers who want to have part-time jobs in order to spend more time raising their children.

Another thing Christians might do to help mothers who have to work outside the home is to get their churches involved in job creation. It is possible for churches to initiate entrepreneurial programs to provide jobs that will allow mothers to stay with their children. For instance, a Black pastor in Richmond, Virginia, has worked out a plan whereby single mothers of his congregation have been trained to repair irons, toasters, and other household appliances in their own homes. With the help of some teachers from a nearby vocational school, the pastor saw to it that these women were trained in the techniques and procedures necessary for repairing household appliances. The equipment necessary to do the repairs was provided by donations from church members. And the pastor himself coordinated the marketing of the services provided by these women. Through his creative efforts, a number of women have been able to earn a decent living and at the same time be available for their children.

At Eastern College, where I teach, a very creative graduate program has been established which specializes in preparing MBA students to set up cottage industries. One of our students has just gotten a welfare mother started in making the uniforms required for the students of a nearby Christian school. This simple beginning may have long-term consequences, not only for the mother making the uniforms, but for her children as well. I am hopeful that in years to come scores of our graduates will discover and help model new ways for mothers to earn a fair income while still providing the kind of personal care that is best for their children. I look forward to the time when many of my students will be creators of cottage industries which will rescue thousands from the dire dilemma of trying to give quality time to mothering while still earning a decent income.

I hope that by this point I have given sufficient evidence that there are forces at work today that make parenting, and particularly mothering, a sometimes overwhelming responsibility. Furthermore, I hope I have provided some insight as to why some young mothers might look for escape from these responsibilities. But still, in all of my arguments, I have either stated or implied that the problem of caring for children is primarily a woman's task. I have argued as though I believed that mothers are somehow better than fathers when it comes to meeting the affectional needs of children. While I have called upon husbands to break from traditional role patterns and to get involved in raising their children, and while I have urged men to take on household tasks hitherto considered woman's work, there is still, in all that I have presented, a not-too-subtle implication that rearing preschool children should be primarily done by mothers. There is an underlying tone in what I have presented that biology is destiny for mothers, and that the ties between mothers and children assign to mothers a unique and essential role which no one else can fill.

This is a somewhat correct assumption. I *do* believe that there are certain social inevitabilities that come from giving birth to babies. During the nine months of pregnancy, I am convinced, the mother and the child interact with each other in ways that imprint the child for life. There is growing evidence that from the time the brain of a developing child becomes active (between eight and ten weeks after conception), there is meaningful communication going on between the mother and the child. That communication, though nonverbal, is nevertheless profound. During the prenatal period, the developing child registers the emotions experienced by the mother and, in all likelihood, certain forms of "imprinting" take place which may determine the psychological orientation of the child for years to come.

What is developing in the mother's womb is an emerging person whose sense of well-being is dependent on the one who bears him or her. In a sense, the socialization and humanization of the child begins prior to birth. For purely biological reasons, the mother is the first and most powerful influence on the developing child.

It is because of my beliefs in the prenatal interaction between mother and child that I contend it is essential that the mother be the primary nurturing agent in the first few years after birth. It seems to me that the transition from the child's emotional world being totally tied up with the mother to the child's being able to involve others in his or her emotional world should be a gradual one. For a mother to abruptly turn over the primary care of her infant child to others, especially during the first three years following birth, seems to me to be dangerous for the well-being of the child. (See Burton L. White, *The First Three Years of Life.*) Fathers are an essential and early part of the young child's enlarging emotional world, but I believe that there are special emotional needs which only mothers, because of their prenatal influence on children, must meet.

The time has come for America to change its values with regard to raising children. If we are to have healthy, happy citizens in the future, we must give primary attention to the raising of boys and girls in this generation. We must convince parents that rearing children deserves a higher priority than do careerism and professional advancement. As a society, we must give to mothering the prestige and honor it deserves. Parents must be convinced that sacrifices are in order during their children's preschool years. Parenting must be lauded as a godly and noble calling. Mothers and fathers should be made to understand that this calling is worthy of limiting career aspirations or even interrupting careers.

The lifespan of Americans is longer than it has ever been, leaving plenty of time for parents to pick up and develop their careers after their children have been carried through the critical and crucial early years of development. I fully believe it is reasonable for mothers to disengage from their careers while their children are going through preschool experiences. They should be on hand to meet those emotional and psychological needs of children which only they can meet. And fathers should not only offer support and encouragement to the mothers of their own children; they should be leaders in the movement to demand that society in general do what is necessary to enable mothers of preschoolers to be at home with their children. To allow the precious early childhood years of children to slip away because of the demands of office or classroom seems sinful.

My daughter went to law school at the University of Pennsylvania. During her time at the university, there were many discussions and lectures aimed at helping the would-be female lawyers figure out how to balance the demands of their careers in law with the demands that go with mothering small children. I asked my daughter what she had concluded after all the talk on this topic. She told me, with some regret on her part, that the obvious conclusion was that something had to give. After hours of discussion and reflection, she had come to realize that nobody can do both mothering of preschool children and full-time "lawyering" adequately at the same time. The demands of each role create tensions with the other. My daughter readily acknowledged that during a child's preschool years, either good mothering or good lawyering would have to suffer.

Those magazine articles about superwomen who somehow manage to fulfill brilliantly and simultaneously the obligations of both careers and motherhood are probably more fiction than reality. It is a mistake not to recognize limitations. Mothering, if done right, is a demanding responsibility which requires great energy and intelligence and is, in and of itself, a full-time career. It is possible, and maybe even beneficial to all concerned, that mothers have part-time jobs in order to enhance their lives and/or earn some extra money. But caring for children should always be treated as the primary responsibility of mothers, and nothing should be allowed to detract from that task.

Fathers must be prepared to make sacrifices, too. Unfortunately, children usually come into their lives just when they think that they should be putting extra time into their careers. In their late twenties and early thirties, many new fathers think that their primary obligation is to make the "right moves" for advancement in their jobs or promotions. Consequently, during the preschool years of their children, they often are not available to help in child care. Too often prolonged work-related absences from home keep fathers from developing good relationships with their small children.

A teaching colleague of mine and his wife have modeled the kind of sacrifices that I think ought to be made by both parents for the sake of their children. He was in graduate school working toward his doctorate when his children were born. There was much pressure on him from the administrators of the college to finish his degree and to get on with developing his career. But my friend knew that he was a father first and a college professor second. He did a good job at teaching, but he delayed completing his doctorate until he felt his family could handle the extra time investment these studies required.

His wife, a highly educated woman of great intelligence, also sacrificially committed herself to making mothering a full-time career. Our college pays rather modest salaries to the faculty, so the fact that she was not gainfully employed meant that the family had to lower its standard of living. This was especially difficult since, because of the location of the college, they are required to live in one of the wealthiest suburbs of Philadelphia. They certainly could have used the extra money she could have earned.

This couple did what they had to do in order to be the kind of parents they thought they ought to be. By some standards, their income forced their family of five to live below the poverty level. But they believed that time and affection were more necessary provisions for a family than owning their own home or having the money to buy things that many Americans have been manipulated into thinking are necessities. I wish more families would accept such a model.

We Christians ought to know better, but most of us are, contrary to Scripture (Rom. 12:1) conformed to this world. We are far too ready to believe that we have to have all the accouterments that go with the media-prescribed "good life"—even when the extra time spent in getting the money for these things causes our children to lose something more precious than what we buy for them. Parenting requires more sacrifices than most of us realize or are willing to make.

For those who have no choice in the matter and are forced out of economic necessity to work full time, there is the hope that you will be able to find some creative ways to make the most of the time you are able to spend with your children. Consider setting up a business in your home. Taking in typing jobs, setting up a telephone answering service, writing, and providing tutoring services are some ways in which mothers have found it possible to be at home with their small children while still carving out a decent living. But if you must be away from your children because of a full-time job, make the best of what I believe to be a very bad situation. Treasure your time with your child, understanding that your presence and attention mean far more than ironed clothes, a clean house, or even teaching a Sunday school class. If there is pain in knowing that you cannot provide the ideal situation, there is joy in realizing that you have every right to make quality time with your child your top priority insofar as it is possible during those very early years.

And to those mothers who do *not* have to be away from their children during their early formative years, realize how fortunate you are, and do not squander your precious opportunity. All too soon, your children will grow up and be gone. When that time comes, you will want to know down deep inside that you did for them the best that you could.

Christopher Lasch, in his book, *The Culture of Narcissism,* contends that children are growing up hostile because they are suffering from emotional deprivation experienced in their early years of development. He is concerned lest this hostility express itself in ways that will make the world a more and more violent place. His arguments are based on some neo-Freudian theories that many question. But, if he is right, the future of the planet may depend on our ability to make the sacrifices that must be made if we are to give our children the loving attention they need to grow into Christlike persons. If we want children who will rise up and call us blessed, we must be willing to pay the price. May it never be said of us that in the pursuit of power, prestige, and material goods we neglected the most important obligation to the next generation and failed to give them the time they needed and deserved.

But, rather than coming at this subject from a negative perspective, my hope is that mothers will see the positive side of being the primary caregiver as a child develops during the preschool years.

Think of what it means to be there when the child takes his or her first steps. Consider the importance of teaching the first words to become part of your child's vocabulary. And most important, think of the thrill that comes from being that special person who is the primary playmate for a small child who is looking for someone with whom to share the joy of life. Why let somebody else have all this fun with our kids? Isn't this what we have them for?[1]

[1]Two studies that were given special attention in this chapter are *A Longitudinal Study of Children with Varying Quality Day Care Experiences,* by Deborah Lowe Vandell, V. Kay Henderson and Kathy Shores Wilson; and *Variations in Early Child Care: Do They Predict Subsequent Emotional and Cognitive Differences?* by Deborah Lowe Vandell and Mary Anne Corasaniti. Both of these studies can be obtained by writing to the Program in Psychology, University of Texas at Dallas, Richardson, Texas 75080. These studies also have excellent bibliographies to provide additional reading on the subject.

5. *What do I do if I'm sexually starved?*

I WAS ONCE on a religious retreat with a group of men. Following an intense and meaningful session in which the retreat speaker made a powerful plea for sexual purity, a small group of us gathered for bedtime devotions. One of the men, a twenty-nine-year-old bachelor who had been particularly agitated by the events of the evening, used this devotional time for confession and prayer. We all sat in stark silence as he told us about his sexual hungers and his attempts to handle them. He was guilty of neither adultery nor fornication. But he went on to tell us tearfully that he did make use of both pornography and masturbation to meet his sexual needs.

When this young man finished pouring out his sexual troubles, he asked us to pray for him. Specifically, he asked that the Lord would take away his sexual hungers so that he would not be tempted to pornographic entertainment or to masturbation again.

At that point I had to interrupt his confessions and pleas. "Just a minute," I said, "I don't think you realize what you're asking. Do you really want to have your sexual appetite cut to nothing? Do you realize that if such a prayer is answered, you won't be *you* anymore? Don't you accept the fact that God gave you your sexual drive because He believed it to be good? Of course the Bible teaches that having a wife for a sexual partner is the way God intends for guys like you to release your pent-up sexual energies. But if you didn't have an intense sexual drive, you might lose one very good reason for getting married."

"But I'm not married!" he answered. "And what's worse, I have no prospects. As a Christian, I shouldn't be doing what I am doing to get release. This sex thing is nothing but a lot of suffering for me."

What this young bachelor agonized about is more common among religious people than most of us either suspect or admit. Living in a society that bombards us with sexually stimulating media messages, and being conditioned by a cultural media permeated with neo-Freudian psychology, most singles are either preoccupied with sex or made to feel there is something wrong with them if they are not. It is all good and well to tell such single Christians that the Bible affirms celibacy and even encourages it as a lifestyle. It sounds very noble to declare that celibacy permits more opportunity for service to God and to others (1 Cor. 7). But for most singles this does not sound like sufficient consolation. They are still left with the frustration of trying to lead a sexually pure life in a sex-saturated society.

But sexual frustration is not just a singles' problem; married people experience it, too! Researchers give ample evidence that a significant proportion of the married population is dissatisfied with the amount of sexual activity in their marriages. More important, there are periods during every marriage when one partner or another feels somewhat unsatisfied with the frequency or intensity of available sexual relations.

Part of this is due to differences between the male and female sex drive. Most males get married between twenty-three and twenty-five years of age, while most females get married between the ages of twenty-one and twenty-three. The problem is that the majority of men experience their most intense sexual interest in their early twenties, just about the time they get married. But women do not reach their sexual peak until they are into their thirties! Unfortunately, by the time most men hit their late thirties, their sexual interest is into a decline.

What all of this means is that during the early stages of marriage, wives may not be as sexually responsive as the husbands would like them to be, and in later years husbands may not be as interested as their wives would like them to be. In such an instance, patience and restraint can be an important expression of love—at times, it may even be the highest expression of love.

Imagine a couple who is experiencing great marital stress because the young husband feels his sexual needs are not being adequately met. Perhaps the wife (let us say she is twenty-three years old) has just had a baby. Prior to the child's birth she just did not feel very sexy. And after the birth, she breast-fed the child, which greatly diminished her sexual appetite. Lacking patience and understanding, the husband decides that because of his wife's failure to attend to his sexual needs, he is justified in looking for "pick ups" who will give him what he wants. Such a man is not a man, but rather a spoiled little boy who has to have what he wants when he wants it. Unfortunately, such a scenario is too often played out in the reality of our egotistic world.

In another possible marital scenario, we might have a wife in her mid-thirties enjoying the height of her sexual interest and drive. Emancipated by some good Christian feminist literature, she has learned that women have sexual rights, too. Her husband, however, is not as amorous as he once was. He is a lawyer working long, exhausting hours as he presses for partnership at his firm. He is nervous about his stage in life and feels a bit threatened by his wife—he has growing doubts about his ability to measure up to her sexual expectations. Often, he deliberately stays up late, hoping that his wife will fall off to sleep before he goes to bed, because he is afraid he will not be able to perform well enough for her. And instead of sympathizing with his plight and expressing appreciation for what he is trying to do, she humiliates him by ridiculing him as sexually inadequate. All the while, there is a female colleague of his at the office who gives him constant affirmation, praising his brilliant legal work and conveying to him that he is an immensely attractive person. The two of them have an affair, which proves to be such an ego lift for this young lawyer that he decides to leave his wife and marry his new flame.

Versions of these fictional accounts are more often played out than most of us realize. It is in this context that the Scriptures tell us:

> The wife hath not power of her own body, but the husband: and likewise also the husband hath not power of his own body, but the wife. Defraud ye not one the other, except it be with consent for a time, that ye may give yourselves to fasting and prayer; and come together again, that Satan tempt you not for your incontinency (1 Cor. 7:4–5).

The trouble is that simple admonishment that we restrain our sexual hungers usually is not enough to solve the problem for most of us—whether we are married or single. We need more help than a simple "Thou shalt not!" We need a practical strategy for dealing with sexual frustration, and I have some suggestions to make about that.

But first, what about the two outlets mentioned at the beginning of this chapter and indulged in by a great many sexually frustrated people—pornography and masturbation?

I firmly believe that in dealing with the problem of sexual frustration, there must be no allowances for pornography. Those who think pornography is a harmless sexual outlet are out of touch with the most modern research and thought on the matter. There is much evidence that pornography is both addictive and progressive.

Many of those who get into pornography discover that they cannot experience sexual arousal without it. I know of one case where a man was so "into" pornography that he had to spend time with the nude photos in *Hustler* magazine in order to get stimulated enough to have sexual relations with his wife. His involvement with pornography had degenerated into an addiction.

Furthermore, there is a growing belief that satiation with one form of pornography creates the need for "harder" forms in order to bring the longed-for "turn ons." In other words, we are finding that those who start with the relatively "soft" porn of the *Playboy* centerfolds often find that after a while they need something more lewd and explicit. My own theoretical perspectives have led me to believe that the eroticism of someone who depends on pornography is tied up with sexual objects which cannot threaten him or her. Hence, the pornographic hungers of such persons finally lead them to get their pleasure from the weakest of all objects—children. I do not believe I am overstating the case when I allege that what begins as a macho thing can end in the sexual exploitation and abuse of little girls and boys. And I contend that the damage that children and society may have to endure from such abuse is too great to allow for any leniency for pornographers, even in the name of free speech.

It took the feminist movement to remind us that our concern with pornography should be not only about what it does to the voyeurs, but also what it does to the objects of their pornographic lusts. The women who pose for pornographic pictures are denigrated and dehumanized. And, of course, this is also true of men and children who pose. There is no way that any Christian can allow for such dehumanization or call it harmless. Every human being has a dignity that comes from being created in the image of God, and to participate in diminishing that dignity is a sin against Him.

When Alfred Kinsey made his famous sex studies in the early 1950s, pornography was essentially a male perversion. That is no longer the case. Over the past thirty years, women have been drawn into the eroticism of pornography and now there is evidence that many of them are also becoming addicted. It is important for us to recognize that women in the church are having hang-ups on pornography and that we must not treat it as an exclusively male problem.

I believe that the church has to do a lot more, both *about* pornography and *for* those who are addicted to it. It is not enough to picket porn shops and legislate massage parlors out of existence. The church must do something for those who have become dependent on pornography. One idea would be to sponsor support groups on the order of Alcoholics Anonymous. Christian leaders could initiate "Pornographers Anonymous" groups, so that individuals who have been seduced into a pornographic lifestyle might find brothers or sisters in Christ who can help strengthen them against temptation. The good news is that anti-pornography groups are becoming aware of this need and are beginning to respond to it. Hopefully, in the near future, such support groups will be available for all those who need help.

Masturbation is still another problematic escape used by many Christians who are sexually frustrated. Empirical studies suggest that most Christian young adults practice masturbation, and that it is very common among Christians who are divorced or widowed.

The Catholic church has long condemned masturbation, calling it "the sin of Onan." In the Old Testament, Onan "wastes his seed" (that is, his semen) and thus incurs the wrath of God:

> And Onan knew that the seed should not be his; and it came to pass, when he went in unto his brother's wife, that he spilled it on the ground, lest that he should give seed to his brother. And the thing which he did displeased the Lord: wherefore he slew him also (Gen. 38:9–10).

Personally, I have never felt that this argument against masturbation was particularly convincing, since Onan's "seed" was wasted by interrupting sexual intercourse rather than by masturbating.

There are many Christian ethicists who believe that masturbation is a completely acceptable way for Christians to gain release from pent-up sexual energies. And certainly masturbation is not as bad as adultery or fornication. If it is a sin at all, consider that there is a difference between sexual sins which involve others and may cause others to fall and those which only involve one's self.

Perhaps the most common Christian argument against the practice of masturbation is that it generates fantasies of illicit sexual practices. There are many who contend that Christian purity of heart (Matt. 5:8) requires that we be free from the fantasies that come while masturbating, that we should allow only pure images to pass through our minds.

There is no doubt that masturbation usually involves fantasies, but I am not convinced that all fantasizing is sin. It seems to me that it is what we decide to do with our fantasies that can cause the problems. If we decide to nurture and preserve our fantasies so that they become preoccupations, and if we begin to entertain ideas of really carrying them out, then I believe they become sinfully destructive.

Sexual fantasies can certainly be temptations, but temptations in and of themselves are not sin. The Bible tells us that Jesus Himself was "in all points tempted like we are," but it goes on to say that He never yielded to temptation (Heb. 4:15). It is what we do with our temptations that make for sin. If we will for them to be realized, we have crossed the line.

Sigmund Freud once said that what we deny by day, we dream of by night. Undoubtedly, he was right on this point. Whether we masturbate or not, whether we will to or not, we will all have some sexual fantasies; they are a natural part of our biological/psychological makeup. Consequently the case against masturbation that is built on the claim that the fantasies it generates are sinful has questionable validity.

On the other hand, the Bible *does* advise us to flee temptation (James 4:7). It can and should be argued that we ought not to encourage temptation to be regularly present, especially when we find ourselves sexually starved. On these grounds, masturbation *could* lead to fantasies which might weaken our resolve for sexual purity, and there may be grounds for calling the practice into question.

So if pornography and masturbation are not acceptable outlets for our sexual urges, what can we do with our sexual hungers that cannot be satisfied? My first suggestion is an old one that I believe we don't consider seriously enough. I believe we need what the neo-Freudian psychologists have called "sublimating activities." Quite simply put, we need things to do which will enable us to expend our sexual energies in spiritually constructive ways.

This is a time-honored way of dealing with sexual frustration—one that our current cultural over-emphasis on sex tends to ignore. I have no way of knowing this, but I believe it is quite possible that Mother Teresa of Calcutta has found an outlet for her sexual energies in her love for the poor of the world. I believe that finding Jesus in the faces of the dying gutter people of Calcutta is a wonderful way to dissipate one's sexual drive in ways that bring glory to God and great personal satisfaction.

St. Teresa, the sixteenth-century mystic after whom Mother Teresa is named, discovered holiness in her erotic love responses to Christ. St. Teresa learned the ecstasy that can come from being in Christ and having Christ in her. I do not fault her as some of my more puritan Protestant friends might do. I believe St. Teresa's love for Christ was holy, but I also believe that the famous woman who now bears her name has found an even better way. Mother Teresa loves Jesus through and in other people. She finds the ultimate gratification for her life in the Christ who waits to greet her in each and every poor and diseased person she loves and serves. Spiritual love *can* compensate for physical drives. Loving service is a form of sublimation that I believe can bring the flesh under control.

Those of us who are lesser Christians need not feel that our spirituality must measure up to Mother Teresa's in order to use this way of sublimating our sexual desires. If we but give it a chance, each of us can find a dissipation of our sexual energies in the opportunities that are everywhere at hand to love the needy and the unlovable in the name of Christ. This is not an unrealistic proposal nor an inadequate escape. We must all be willing to be taught by Scripture, which tells us:

> There hath no temptation taken you but such as is common to man; but God is faithful, who will not suffer you to be tempted above that ye are able; but will with the temptation also make a way to escape, that ye may be able to bear it (1 Cor. 10:13).

Harry is a divorced man. Furthermore, he has serious questions about whether or not the Bible allows grounds for divorced persons to remarry. He has the sexual drives of most young men in their early thirties, and those drives could easily prove conducive to sin. But Harry has committed himself to working with poor inner-city people. Day in and day out, he spends incredible energy in his daily round of activities. He counsels countless teenagers, organizes sports programs, conducts Bible studies, works with problem parents, carries out door to door evangelism, and directs cultural enrichment programs for children. He supervises an enthusiastic staff of workers who are fed by his love for people and his energetic style of service.

What Harry does is not simply an escape from his real sexual self. It is a gratifying lifestyle that enables him to compensate for his lack of sexual gratification. He readily admits to having the normal sexual urges for a man of his age, but the gratification forthcoming from his service to others makes his sexual deprivation bearable. It is safe to say that Harry's sexual energies are being successfully sublimated. That doesn't mean he doesn't experience occasional frustration—but the frustration he experiences is something he is able to handle in a positive way.

It is not necessary to become a missionary nor to become a Mother Teresa in order to sublimate sexual energies. But it is important that your primary vocation in life be emotionally gratifying. This is an important point that is not always recognized. If the job you have to go to day in and day out is one that leaves you psychologically fulfilled, then you will find that your level of sexual frustration will be greatly diminished.

Erich Fromm, in his now-old but still very significant book, *The Art of Loving,* provides an extensive argument supporting the claim that a great deal of sexual frustration and sexual deviance results from jobs that leave workers without a sense of having done anything creative or of having produced anything that has contributed to the good or well-being of others.

I have often used this insight from Fromm when counseling sexually frustrated persons. In one particular case, I was working with a man who worked in a factory that manufactured cigarettes. Not only was his job extremely routine, leaving no room for creativity and skill, but he was well aware of the fact that what he was helping to produce brought expensive addiction and even death to a lot of people.

As we talked, I was able to help this man see that there might be some connection between his failure to get gratification from his work and his lack of satisfactory sexual fulfillment in his marriage. Little by little he came to recognize that the feelings of dissatisfaction and emptiness which he was blaming on his sex life were really being caused by what was happening to him at work.

This story has a happy ending. The man quit his job and became an automobile mechanic. He had confessed to me that he had always wanted to be a mechanic but had never had the training to get into that line of work. However, with some urging from his wife and me, he went to night school and learned the trade he had always wanted. Today he is one of those wonderful honest mechanics who make life easier for a great number of people. And, yes, the gratification provided from his job did wonders for his sex life.

The argument may sound strange, but I believe that Fromm is essentially right. If you are sexually uptight and frustrated, it may be that you are trying to use sexual gratification to compensate for feelings of estrangement and emptiness that come from a meaningless job. Perhaps it is difficult for you to change jobs, but if your work leaves you emotionally and psychologically dissipated, you are foolish not to make a Herculean effort to do so. Staying in a job you despise can easily lead to sexual destruction.

If you cannot change jobs, no matter how much you want to, then it is important that you spend a good bit of your spare or leisure time doing creative and fulfilling things. A hobby may suffice, but it is more likely that the void you feel can be filled only by doing something that will bless others.

Perhaps you should talk with your pastor about some ways that might enable you to make a major contribution to the good of others. For all of its faults, the church still has more options for making important contributions to the well-being and salvation of others than any other institution. Churches have a multiplicity of service opportunities, from visiting the sick and lonely to teaching Sunday school classes, which can give you a chance to make a wonderful difference in this world.

There are also opportunities outside the church. The local Habitat for Humanity chapter can provide you with a chance to help poor people afford decent housing. Hospitals, ecology groups, and political movements need volunteers. Just look around; there is plenty of meaningful work that needs doing. Volunteer to work for something in which you believe. You are needed, and who knows, in your good deeds you might be finding deliverance from one of your worst temptations.

Understanding and sublimation of the sexual urge are essential at every stage of life. Recent research indicates that most of us will be sexually active (or at least sexually interested) throughout most of our lives. Actually, a seventy-year-old woman can have pretty much the same sexual propensity as a seventeen-year-old woman. This may be shocking news to those who think that all of that stuff is packed away after middle age. But as a middle-aged man who sometimes wonders what his wife will be like in her old age, I say, "Hooray!"

The down side of this news is that male sexual interest and drive diminish greatly in later years. But all is not lost. Researchers tell us that, with a properly sympathetic partner, a man can remain sexually active until the day he dies. The wife may not get all that she wants sexually from her husband in their golden years, but love can cover a multitude of inadequacies and leave both partners content with life.

When all is said and done in the matter of sexual frustration, it has mostly been said. All the good ideas about sublimation may not solve your problem adequately. You just may find that you have to live with some level of sexual frustration for the rest of your life and that you may not be the totally satiated person that the self-help books sold at airport bookstores promise that you can be. However, it is time to realize that there is no such thing as a completely satisfied person, anyway. Otherwise, there would be no need for heaven. We only get a piece of the pie. There is always something more that we want out of life that we cannot have. In the face of that reality, we must learn to put up with what we cannot change. It is possible to survive even without all the sex we want. Frustration is not torture. We can still live relatively satisfying lives even if all our sexual hungers are not satiated. There are other things in life, and those who do not think so are not only wrong but sick. In this world you will meet great sexual temptations and maybe even great sexual frustration. But be of good cheer. The good news of the gospel is that He has overcome what you will encounter in the world. With His help you can handle *not* getting what you want and still be happy.

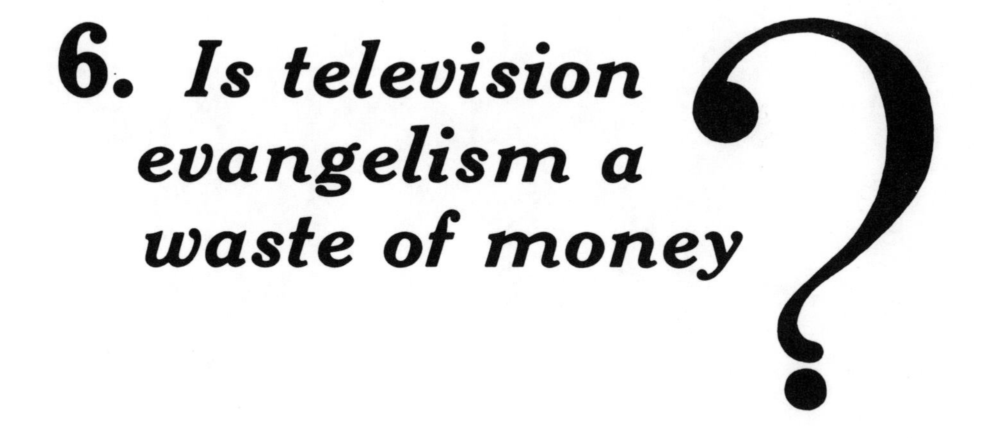

6. *Is television evangelism a waste of money?*

IF CHILDHOOD IS THAT TIME IN LIFE when certain ugly realities are as yet unknown, then television has, as social critic Neil Postman suggests, abolished childhood for twentieth-century Americans. Today, every boy and girl in America knows about rape, incest, and AIDS. These subjects, and others just as shocking, are a standard part of everyday television programming. Television has abolished childhood because it does not allow society to keep anything secret from children anymore.

But children are not the only ones who have been hurt by television; TV has done a job on us all. An Amishman once asked me why we "people of the world" did not first find out what television would do to us before we let it into our homes? I did not know how to answer him. It *is* rather stupid for those of us who are Christians to so readily allow viewpoints and values which are diametrically opposed to our beliefs to come pouring into our homes packaged as entertainment.

The number of murders and sexual assaults which television makes a part of the daily viewing fare of many Christian families is appalling. There is no need for me to cite all the depressing statistics about television violence and amorality in order to make the point. Furthermore, what is *not* negative on television is often asinine. We have watched stupid stuff for so long that we are no longer capable of evaluating how idiotic some of it really is.

Recently I was watching television with some visitors from the hills of Burma. As I sat with them, I began to ask myself what impressions they were getting of America from the TV shows that were on. My speculation as to how things might appear to them made me strongly aware of how ridiculous the shows must seem. And I concluded that the shows *were* ridiculous. I became embarrassed over the fact that I, along with millions of other Americans, was watching so much superficial and in some cases even obscene, broadcasting every day.

In the face of the content of most of what comes across in the secular media, many Christians welcomed the idea of Christian TV. As a teenage boy I remember watching one of the very first

Christian television shows, "Youth on the March," which featured a Philadelphia evangelist named Percy Crawford. This grandfather of Christian television broadcasting is long since gone, but what he started has expanded far beyond what he could ever have imagined. "Youth on the March" was watched by Christians who were hungry for some good entertainment. There were evangelicals across the nation who longed for shows which would not violate their moral sensitivities. Many welcomed the opportunity to watch and listen to Christian musicians who could belt out the old gospel favorites they had come to love.

There is no doubt that Christian television has provided some fun entertainment for the religious community. But when the claim is made, as it often is by one prominent televangelist, that television is the best and most powerful means of communicating the gospel to a lost world, I grow very cynical and skeptical. This same evangelist claims that if Jesus were among us in the flesh today, He would make television His primary instrument for getting His message out to the world. To such statements I must strongly object.

On a number of occasions when I have had the opportunity to address large audiences, I have taken an informal survey to see how people have come to know Jesus. I ask how many became Christians as the result of listening to some Christian radio show. Seldom does a hand go up. When I ask how many were saved through a Christian television show, the response is not much better. Out of a crowd of several thousand people, usually just a few hands go up when I ask how many have become Christians because of a sermon they heard. Usually only two or three percent of the crowd responds.

But when I ask how many have become Christians because some person loved them and shared the gospel with them, the response is always overwhelming. There is never any doubt after such surveys that the best and most "powerful" means of evangelism is not TV at all, but ordinary people who love their friends and relatives enough to tell them about Christ.

In light of this evidence about how evangelism is best carried out, it is difficult to warrant the expenditure of hundreds of millions of dollars annually to sponsor Christian television on the assumption that it is a primary instrument of evangelism. I believe that this money would be better spent in feeding the hungry, caring for the homeless, giving medical care to the desperately poor in Third-World countries, providing education for illiterate children in the world's urban slums, and underwriting the ministries of the thousands of "barefoot evangelists" who travel from village to village in Africa and Asia.

In no way am I suggesting that Christian programs be taken off the air. Instead, I am proposing that they be funded another way. Those who put on these shows should try to raise the money that they need for broadcasting through the selling of advertising time. I find nothing wrong with commercial advertising being interjected into television programs featuring Christian singers and entertainers. Of course, the kinds of commercials acceptable for religious programming would have to be chosen carefully. But thirty years ago Bishop Fulton Sheen was able to solve this problem by utilizing "appropriate" commercials to finance his prime-time major network show.

I am not sure that preaching should be bracketed by commercial advertisements, but then again it is already so bracketed to some extent. Consider the fact that often things like Christmas tree ornaments or gift items are offered by televangelists to encourage people to send in financial contributions. The "special offers" that come before and after their sermons seem no more or less worldly than some of the more strictly commercial ads.

I hope that no one takes my critique of religious TV as a blanket condemnation of what televangelists do. I have been on some religious television talk shows myself. Furthermore, I enjoy some of the Christian programs that are regularly broadcast across the country. It is just that I view most of these shows as Christian entertainment and am somewhat doubtful about whether they are deserving of the hundreds of millions of dollars contributed by people who believe that TV is an effective means of evangelism.

Even with this statement, I must exercise some caution because it seems as though the television sermons of Billy Graham have affected many people. However, there is a consensus among most evangelicals that Billy Graham is in a class all by himself, and that what is true for him may not be true for the rest of us. For some reason, Graham seems to possess an effectiveness that the others lack. A majority of those who have been converted because of television sermons cite Graham's sermons as the ones which reached them. But even in those cases where people say they have been reached by Billy Graham's sermons, there is evidence that the sermons alone were not the primary factor in the decision-making process. In most instances, people who were led to Christ by television sermons were watching the show with Christians who, prior to and following the show, expressed love and gave backup explanations of the meaning of salvation. Consequently, it is uncertain whether the sermons or the Christian friends were what was crucial.

One of my primary concerns about television evangelism is that many of the programs (such as "The 700 Club") are laden with political views. There is nothing wrong with Christians having political viewpoints and making them public. However, in almost every case I know, the political views expressed on Christian television shows are conservative Republican views. It seems as though there is something wrong and a bit unconstitutional when perspectives which represent the interests of one political party can be broadcast on TV, financed by contributions that are made as tax-deductible religious gifts. Simply speaking, money given to support particular views of conservative Republicans *or* liberal Democrats should not be tax deductible. Those gifts should be treated like any other contribution to a political cause or candidate.

Recently, for instance, Jerry Falwell has been giving a great deal of time on his television show, "The Old Time Revival Hour," to solicit funds and signatures in an attempt to get a pardon for Col. Oliver North, the hero/culprit of the Iran arms deal. It is not my place to decide either the guilt or innocence of Col. North. But it *is* my responsibility to object to this partisan political issue getting television time that has been paid for with money that was tax deductible on the grounds it was given for religious purposes.

Conservative Republicanism is a very viable political option for evangelical Christians, but it is not the only option. Unfortunately, most people in secular society, because of what they have seen on Christian television shows, have come to think that all evangelical Christians are part of the New Right. Actually, there are many evangelicals who identify with the political left. I myself am chairman of the board of directors for Evangelicals for Social Action, an organization made up of thousands of evangelical leaders across the country who identify with a host of positions many might consider "liberal." Most of us in ESA stand in opposition to many of the proposals that political conservatives would make on military spending. Many of us would advocate the creation of a Palestinian state as part of an overall solution to the settlement of hostilities in the Middle East. We take a strong position against the Botha government in South Africa and have been in opposition to the Contras in Nicaragua.

All of these positions would be condemned by politically conservative televangelists who contend that their political opinions are based on biblical teachings. But what those televangelists must recognize is that many of us who differ with them also believe *our* opinions are based on the Word of God; we just differ in what we think the Bible prescribes as a means for achieving peace and justice. We are just as committed to traditional Christian theology and Biblical inerrancy as our conservative brothers and sisters. They have no right to suggest that those who oppose them in politics are somehow less evangelical than they are.

Regrettably, televangelists have the power to convince the rest of the world through their television programs that evangelicalism and conservative politics necessarily go together. This puts those of us evangelicals who are "liberal" on certain issues in an awkward situation. Personally, I think that it is a mistake to ally evangelicalism with any one particular political party or ideology. I believe that within the evangelical fold there should be a variety of political options for those who want to work out their convictions in governmental policy.

My final concern about televangelism arises from what the experts in the sociology of communications say about how the medium of television shapes the way we are able to proclaim the gospel. Scholars such as Marshall McLuhan have pointed out that television is not neutral; it conditions what we try to communicate through it. McLuhan and others have convincingly argued that the television medium requires all that is broadcast to be packaged in small, entertaining units. As a case in point, the news has been transformed into an array of stories, each of which must be told in a short forty-five-second slot and presented in an entertaining manner. Television as a medium for communication does not lend itself to in-depth analysis. "Action News" is the order of the day. Nothing that is complex or involved is put on the evening news. The stories that *are* put on the air are those that can be reduced to punch lines and pictures. Obviously, such limitations necessitate distortion.

What many of us have not grasped is that the televising of the gospel message results in the same sorts of distortions. The complex dimensions of biblical truth must be ignored in religious television broadcasting. The gospel must be reduced on the one hand to what can be seen and reduced to one-sentence aphorisms on the other. It is therefore no wonder that most of what is on religious television reflects charismatic forms of Christianity. Healing services are highly visual and make for good television viewing. There is nothing that is difficult to understand in charismatic healing services. Sick people are made well. It is easy enough to say "Jesus can heal you!" If the healings can be broadcast live, all the better. There is no way that viewers will endure a well-developed theological explanation of what God can and cannot do. There is no need for such involved presentations. What God can do is reduced to a simple process of "show and tell."

The main problem with all of this is that there is much evidence that what is at the core of Christ's message gets left out. It is hard to reduce the meaning of the cross to an amusing forty-five-second spot. You can show a crucifixion in that time, but it is impossible to get to the depth of the cross in that manner. It is difficult to communicate in a convincing way to the viewing audience that there are blessings to be gained by giving up all that you have for the poor, and that there is joy in being persecuted for righteousness' sake.

Consequently, by trial and error most televangelists have found that what broadcasts well is a prosperity theology that promises wealth and good fortune to all who believe. In the hands of the best televangelists, Christianity becomes the biggest and best give-away show on television. It is better than "Wheel of Fortune" because everyone can get in on the prizes. The Holy Spirit comes off better than Vanna White because on television He assures that everyone will be a winner. Those who send in prayer requests (in most cases with financial contributions to the ministry enclosed) can be the recipients of better jobs and new cars. Those who trust in the Jesus who is broadcast via television can have all kinds of good things just by naming them and claiming them. Health, wealth, and happiness offered in small amazing segments is what programs well on television, so that is how television tends to portray Christianity.

The medium, says McLuhan, is the message. And he is right. If the nature of the medium lends itself to simplistic amusement, then the Man of Sorrows with all of His profundity must adapt when He comes across the television screen. It is not surprising that when Malcolm Muggeridge was asked how we can use television to broadcast the message of Christ, he simply answered, "You can't!" Television contradicts what Christianity is about in its deepest essence. Television can entertain, but it takes a Person to bid us come and die.

I find it difficult to deal with television evangelism without being far too sweeping in my generalizations. I have spent many good hours watching television preachers. My life has been enriched by much of what I have seen and heard on Christian programs via the electronic media. Of all my concerns, my primary discomfort has been with the means of financing these shows. What often has to be done to keep these programs on the air can lead to the gross misrepresentation of Christianity, although I am sure that such is not the intention of those who develop these programs. Perhaps a great deal of new creative thought should be put into coming up with ways to finance these programs.

Some interesting steps are already being taken in that direction. For instance, in Canada there is one nationwide program that depends on a relatively small group of lay persons who completely underwrite all the expenses of the program, rendering appeals on the air unnecessary. In the Chicago area, there is a very fine program that is of sufficiently high quality to warrant being on the Public Broadcasting System with no charge for airtime. Perhaps the Christian Broadcasting Network could make enough money from commercial advertising on those programs *not* directly religious in nature to cover the expenses of those programs that *are* of a direct religious nature.

Television is here to stay. Those who think we can escape its negative influences simply by turning off our sets ignore the reality that our whole culture is being molded by the medium. There is no escape. We cannot get away from television. We must learn to live with it—and if possible—use it in positive ways. Mr. Rogers learned to use it for kids. We ought to be at least half as creative in finding ways to use it for overtly religious broadcasting.

7. *Should we pull our kids out of the public school system?*

IT MIGHT BE BEST simply to respond to the question of pulling kids out of public schools by saying that "it all depends." My wife and I have two grown children. We wish that we had sent one of them to a Christian secondary school and believe that the other one benefited by being in the public school system. Hindsight is always easy, and at the time we faced the question of where it would be best for our children to go to high school, we did what we thought was right. And we did pray about our decision. But in retrospect, we are not sure whether we made the right decision.

The advantages of having kids in Christian schools are well known. First of all, children tend to be very much impressed by their teachers, and at certain ages they find them to be more of a source of truth and authority than their own parents. All of us who are parents remember our children countering something we said with the simple assertion, "My teacher says . . . ." Since so much of what children believe and think is determined by their teachers, it is probably important that those teachers be Christians.

Second, boys and girls have their basic world view heavily influenced, if not determined, by their school experiences. Whether or not they view life as having any meaning or purpose, whether or not they see any moral order to the universe, whether they view human beings as sacred creations of God or simply as animals which have evolved more or less by accident, are all important parts of a world view (or *Weltanschauung*, as sociologists and philosophers would say) which is intellectually hammered out during the formative years of elementary and secondary education. The doctrines of the Christian faith will make sense to young people only if they seem compatible with the world view that they accept as the taken-for-granted reality in which they live. Once we recognize the importance of having a world view that is conducive to faith in God and in the biblical revelation, it seems essential that children develop their world view under the direction of teachers who are themselves Christians. Christian schools can provide assurance that such will be the case.

Third, it can be strongly argued that a wholistic education cannot take place in a school system which, because it is publicly funded by a religiously pluralistic population, must exclude information that might either enhance or denigrate particular religious interests. For example, history classes in a public school system cannot have a thorough discussion of what the Protestant Reformation was all about. In the study of art, much of the great music of Bach, Mozart, and other great composers must either be ignored or understood on a very superficial level because various religious and secular sensitivities have to be respected. Certainly sex education in the public schools, which of necessity require the absence of biblical teachings on such matters, is something quite different from what most Christians would think appropriate. Literature, social problems, and a variety of other subjects have to be carefully censored by public school teachers in order to avoid any kind of religious bias.

Considering such limitations, Christians can justifiably ask if a good education does not necessitate schools which are free to integrate religious faith and academic disciplines. They must ask whether or not they are denying their children a thorough education by placing them in public schools.

Arguments such as these can be articulated with conviction and convincing rhetoric. And added to these arguments are the warnings of the alarmists with whom parents are often confronted and who leave them downright scared of a public school education for their children.

There are those who warn parents that the public school system is propagating an anti-Christian brand of secular humanism. The fact that biology classes often involve the teachings of Darwin's doctrine of evolution, without giving equal time to those creationist teachings that claim God created human beings apart from any process of natural selection, is used as evidence of the anti-Christian bias of the public school curriculum. The removal of Bible reading and prayer from classroom experiences in public schools is deemed by some to be directly related to increases in juvenile delinquency, teenage alcoholism, and drug use. There are some who contend that children in public schools stand a fairly strong chance of having homosexuals as teachers and, therefore may be subverted into alternative sexual lifestyles.

Some of these alarmist arguments reach outlandish dimensions, especially among those extremists who view the entire public school system as having been infiltrated by communists who are trying to take over the country by subverting our children. I never cease to be amazed at how many seemingly reasonable people buy into such alarmist views and end up seeing the public school system as some kind of demonic plot against a supposedly Christian America.

I, for one, am not convinced that the decision of the Supreme Court to remove Bible reading from the public school setting has been quite the disaster that many of my colleagues in the Christian ministry believe that it is. Having attended public school in the Philadelphia school system prior to the Supreme Court's decision on Bible reading and prayer in public schools, I can vaguely remember partaking in those religious exercises. Perhaps there were some impressions being made on me of which I was unaware. But my own recollection of these religious preludes to the time of learning may well justify the claim that the whole thing was counterproductive. I recall other children chatting with each other while the Bible was being read. On many occasions, some student would be assigned the task of reading the Scriptures so that the teacher could take roll while the "religious exercises" (as they were called in my school) were going on. The prayer was uttered with anything but reverence.

All in all, "the religious exercises" as I remember them served to trivialize religion, and the way in which they were carried out made the sacred appear as something that we had to go through but did not need to take seriously. Soren Kierkegaard, the Danish philosopher/theologian, once said, "There are those who tell lies so convincingly that people think they are telling the truth. But far more dangerous, are those who tell the truth in such a way that people think that they are telling a lie." Such was the case in my school experiences with religious exercises. From time to time the teachers would tell us to pay attention to what was going on because it was important. But the manner in which the truth of God was read from the Scriptures left most of us feeling that it was not important at all.

Those who argue in favor of the Scriptures being read in the public school system seem to ignore the consequences this policy can have in places where Christianity and Judaism are not the dominant religions. For instance, in Utah, where Mormonism is the religion of the majority, Christian boys and girls from evangelical churches would have to sit through the reading of the Book of Mormon. I am not sure what kind of impression this would have on them, but I would prefer that they not have to endure it. In Hawaii, where Buddhism is dominant, it might be necessary for Christian kids to have to listen to daily readings from the *Upanishad*.

Personally, I have the feeling that Christian families ought to have Bible reading and prayer in their homes each day before the children ever go off to school. If that is not possible, then some other time should be set aside each day for family Bible study. This would more than compensate for any loss that might have been suffered as a result of the ruling of the Supreme Court regarding religion in the public schools.

Of course the fact that the Bible was not handled properly in my experiences in public school might be one more argument in favor of Christian schools. Children would benefit from time spent in Bible study at school each day regardless of whether or not their parents have family devotions at home. Christian schools could provide that kind of training, which is so essential for setting children on a good course for life. I agree! I just do not think the loss of Bible reading and prayer in the public schools of America is any big deal.

There are certain politicians who have made it a big deal in order to get the evangelical vote. There are some televangelists who have used the issue to raise big money for their ministries by claiming that they could help to save America by putting the Bible back into our public schools. Americans know that something has gone wrong in America and they are afraid of the future. Unfortunately, it is easy for demagogues to play on those fears and gain financial and political support by setting forth the simplistic solution that a few minutes of Bible reading in school will go a long way toward restoring our nation to the spiritual greatness which we think it once had.

One of the meanest arguments against public schools comes from alarmists who contend that public school students can be forced to study under homosexuals and might even be subjected to homosexual seduction. This contention makes me furious—not because I believe there are no homosexuals in the public school system, but because of the implication that homosexuals are some kind of special threat to children. It is about time that those "homophobics" who spread false fears about homosexuals come up with sufficient evidence to prove their claim that these people are particularly dangerous in the classroom. Oh, I do not doubt that the accusers can come up with some isolated instances wherein homosexual teachers have behaved inappropriately with students. But I am sure that, if the whole story were to be told, there would be ample evidence to show that the percentage of *heterosexual* teachers who have seduced their students is greater.

Please do not get me wrong. I think we *should* be wary of the sexual seduction of pupils in the public school system! But I abhor the implication that homosexuals are more dangerous than heterosexuals in this regard. If the facts were known, I think there would be ample evidence that many homosexuals live in such fear of being exposed that they are extremely unlikely to give even hints of misbehavior. We should keep an eye on all teachers; but there is no reason to believe that homosexuals pose a special threat for our children—or, for that matter, that Christian schools are more free of homosexuals than are public schools. Claims that we should pull our kids out of public schools because they are endangered by homosexual teachers are uncalled for and cruel—not to mention unchristian.

Before I go on to cite some of the arguments for keeping our kids in public schools, I want to point out that I am the founder of an urban ministry among poor inner city children which has made the starting of a Christian school an important part of its program. Through the Evangelical Association for the Promotion of Education, we have tried to serve and evangelize boys and girls who live in urban ghettos that are sociological disasters. In some of the communities where we work, more than 70 percent of the children will never even graduate from high school, and most of those who do graduate will be functional illiterates. More than 90 percent of all the pregnancies in one of these ghettos will involve unmarried teenagers. Most of the children in these communities live in single-parent homes. And most of their homes are completely devoid of any Christian teaching. Drugs are everywhere, and the prevailing influences in these communities leave children with little hope of escape from disastrous lives.

For years those who have led our ministry to these inner city children did the traditional things. They conducted Bible clubs, sports programs, Christian summer camps, and so on. Hundreds of boys and girls as well as teenagers made decisions for Christ; our statistics on conversions were remarkable. But as time passed, we recognized that most of those who were converted could not stand up to the anti-Christian pressures which were so much a part of their homes and neighborhoods. These new Christians were easily overwhelmed by the demonic forces which seemed prevalent at every turn.

Out of frustration, we made the decision to start Cornerstone Christian Academy. This school allows us to nurture the boys and girls we have brought to Christ in an atmosphere conducive to a Christian lifestyle and value formation. We consider the ghettos of America to be mission fields, and we consider Cornerstone Christian Academy a mission school. The teachers who teach in this school are viewed as missionaries by their home churches, and some of them even receive financial support from their home churches. We raise the funds to cover the children's tuition by getting them sponsors from affluent suburban churches. We figure that if people are willing to sponsor children to be educated on the foreign mission field (as they are able to do through such organizations as World Vision and Compassion International), then they should be willing to sponsor the education of the children in American urban ghettos who are every bit as much in need of Christian nurture.

We believe that our ministry in Philadelphia should bring us to the point where we can go to those people who run the public school system and tell them we are willing to take their problem children and teenagers. We want to be able to say, "We are the ones who will take the stones which the builders reject, and with them we will lay the cornerstones of new communities in the ghettos." We believe that, as Christians, we should be on hand to pick up those who are the casualties of the system and restore them to what God would have them be.

It is obvious from my description of the reasons behind the creation of Cornerstone Christian Academy that we have been motivated by concerns that are very different from those of most parents who pull their kids out of the public school systems. Perhaps the worst possible motivation for removing children from public schools is to avoid racial integration. When the Supreme Court ruled that public schools had to be integrated, there were some racist "Christians" who responded by pulling their children out of public schools and putting them into racially segregated Christian academies. Utilizing the Sunday school buildings of churches, thousands of these Christian schools came into being overnight. They became the primary instruments for frustrating progress toward the integrated society which should be the goal for all Christians.

Fortunately, times have changed, and so have many of these schools. Many institutions which were started to maintain segregation are now integrated, and racism is no longer the strong motivation for starting Christian schools that it once was. But even though most Christian schools make concerted efforts to foster racial integration in their student constituencies, there are still enough racist "Christian" schools around to prove an embarrassment to those who start Christian schools for the right reasons.

Perhaps the strongest argument against pulling our kids out of public schools and putting them in Christian schools is that this action does severe damage to the public school system. First of all, Christian kids are removed from an educational environment in which their presence is greatly needed. I believe that children can be witnesses for Christ and as such can be a godly leaven in schools. Too often the removal of Christian kids takes the best children out of the school system, leaving teachers with the most difficult children and the poorest students. I realize that there are a lot of value judgments implied in such a statement, but I think empirical studies will back up what I have said.

Second, the parents of Christian children are very much needed in the Parent-Teacher Associations (PTAs) of the public schools to see that decency and good education are encouraged. There is much that can be done by Christians in the public school system that is within the parameters laid down by the Supreme Court regarding separation of church and state. I believe that Christian parents must not abandon the public schools, especially in light of the fact that most poor children will never have the tuition to go to Christian schools even if they want to do so. According to the Free Enterprise Institute in Washington, D.C., 30 percent of all children born in this decade will grow up in poverty, with their only educational options being within the public school system. We Christians cannot just take our own children and run away.

Christian responsibility requires that we stay involved with public school education, even if we feel we must choose private

Christian education for our own children. An example of what can be done is found in Pittsburgh, Pennsylvania, where a group of Christian leaders were determined to make a difference in their public schools. Through a program called "Cities in Schools," they resolved to place Christians as counselors for problem students. School principals were asked to provide office space in their schools for these specially trained Christian counselors. The kids with the worst problems are referred to these counselors. They get the "burnouts" and "druggies." They get the incorrigibles whom the regular school counselors consider beyond help. The results have been remarkable.

Needless to say, these Christian counselors have had to walk a fine line in order not to violate the principle of separation of church and state. They cannot talk about Christ to the kids they counsel as long as they are operating on school grounds during school hours. But these counselors go out of their way to follow up in informal ways on the kids with whom they work in school. On their own time and outside school settings, they are able to bring the spiritual dimension to bear on many lives. The Cities in Schools program is set up in over seventy schools in the Pittsburgh area, and the model is being considered by Christians in other cities of America. Cities in Schools is a brilliant example of concerned Christians who are making a difference in the public school system.

Another way for Christians to influence the lives of young people in the public school system is through making better use of "released time" programming. Contrary to widespread opinion, Christians can set up special Christian training programs on school time. There is a constitutional right to establish a period each week during regular school hours in which boys and girls can be given Christian training and Bible study. If Christians are opposed to what their children might be taught in the sex education classes of public schools, they are entitled to have them removed from those sex education classes and placed in special classes taught by an outside teacher who could communicate Christian values and perspectives on sexual behavior.

Actually, the Supreme Court did not so much run religion out of the public school system as it ruled that children could not be subjected to religious exercises against their wills or the wills of their parents or be embarrassed by having to be excused while others entered into such practices. However, there is nothing to prevent Christians from requesting time when children could be released by the public school system so that Christian education could take place at private expense.

In my view, the reason there is not more of a Christian witness in public schools is not that the Supreme Court prohibits the witness. The reason is that Christians are either too lazy or too uninformed to take advantage of the wonderful opportunities that exist for ministry within the limitations of the law.

Getting back to the consideration of Christian vs. public education for one's own children, I am sure that there are more pros and cons to this issue than I have noted. I have not given a clear resolution to this controversial matter. Any decision must take into consideration the individual child's personality and needs. We have seen that a case for pulling our children out of public schools can be made if we consider the fact that a Christian education provides the best basis for developing a Christian world view, effectively integrating religious faith and academic knowledge, and giving our children teachers who, by living out their Christian faith, provide the kind of role models that will help students establish their own lifestyles as Christians.

On the other hand, there are some important points for parents to consider before making the decision to enroll their children in a private Christian school:

- We must *not* pull our children out of the public school system in order to avoid court-ordered racial integration—or to avoid associating with others who are not like us.
- We must *not* pull our children out of the public school system in order to escape the presence of homosexual teachers.
- We must be ever mindful that the public school system is one of the "principalities and powers" which God sent His Son to redeem and save.

As such, the public school system cannot be abandoned by Christians. We must be committed to transforming our public schools into the kind of system that God would have it to be. Pulling our kids out of the public school system may hinder our ability to be involved in such an effort. Also, the absence of Christian children in the public school system will diminish Christian influence in the classrooms and in extracurricular activities.

One thing is certain—the general quality of public schools must be improved, or people will pull their kids out of them simply to place them in better learning situations. The continual decline of public education should alarm us all, and we need to carefully evaluate whether or not pulling our kids out of public schools will further that decline. As we face the future, we must not only consider what is best for our own children, but what is best for all the children of the world.

However, there must be limits to our commitment to public education. We must not allow our children to be sacrificial lambs in our crusades to improve a school system that is desperately in need of redemptive influences. A dear friend of mine had to face this fact and reluctantly remove his son from a public school to send him to a private Christian school.

My friend's family, along with five other Christian families, had moved into a dilapidated section of Philadelphia with the express purpose of being a people of God whose presence would bear witness to the gospel. He had every expectation that he and his brothers and sisters in Christ could infiltrate the various institutions and organizations of their community and apply the biblical principles of the kingdom of God.

My friend was especially anxious that his son go to the local public school so that he and his family would have the right to challenge the evils and shortcomings that were evident there. What my friend did not anticipate was the price that his son would have to pay for all of this. The boy, who was a deeply sensitive child, was beaten up daily. Gangs preyed on him for protection money. Little by little he became withdrawn and intensely nervous. He regularly had nightmares and gave evidence of being unable to function academically. Finally, my friend and his wife were left with no alternative but to pull him out of the school and place him in a private Christian school where he could learn in safety.

For those who choose to keep their children in public schools, wisdom must be exercised. When the negative effects of the school become too much for the child to handle with confidence, he or she must be removed for protective reasons. This may be a loss to the missionary objectives of the family, but it is crucial to recognize that the parents' first obligation in the propagation of the gospel is the salvation of their own children.

Also, it is important to recognize that Christian schools, even at their best, are not perfect places. Kids in Christian schools can be into drugs and destructive sexual behavior. I know of one family that had to take their child out of a Christian school in order to get her away from some "wild" friends!

Children are unique individuals, and each school has its own particular traits and characteristics. One child might greatly benefit from a public school experience, and it is possible for a child to be "turned off to Christ" in a Christian school where he or she feels that Christianity is being forced upon the students. In giving the pros and cons on this question, I have given no categorical answer, because there is none. No one answer will be right for every child and every school. In the words of the apostle Paul, we must work out our own answers on this issue—as with any issue—with fear and trembling (Phil. 2:12).

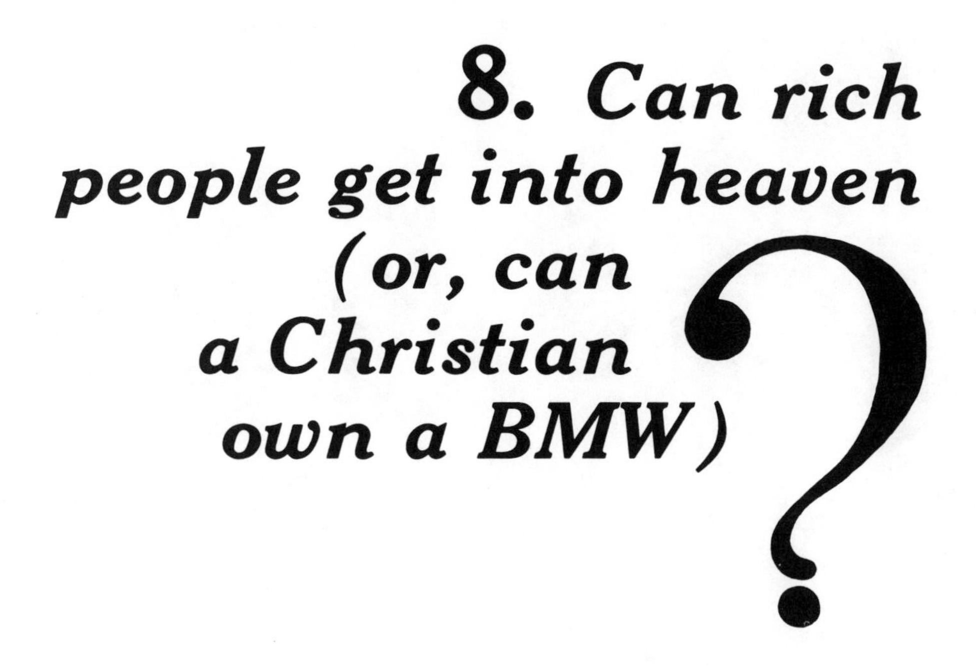

8. *Can rich people get into heaven (or, can a Christian own a BMW)?*

JESUS SAID that it would be hard:

> It is easier for a camel to go through the eye of a needle, than for a rich man to enter into the kingdom of God (Mark 10:25).

In 1984, I was in Africa. I was in the Sahil region just south of the Sahara where drought and desertification (the gradual transformation of arable land into desert) were prevalent and devastating. In village after village, I saw what most of us have seen on those television specials designed to tell us of the suffering of the poor who live in the midst of the African famine. I saw the children with their swollen bellies—swollen, ironically, not because they had eaten too much, but because they had eaten too little. I saw these children, too debilitated from malnutrition and dysentery to brush the flies out of their teary, sick eyes. On that trip, all the sights which have become familiar via those late night TV shows that promote the child sponsorship programs of Compassion International, World Vision, and others became living realities to me.

In such a situation, one instinctively tries to accept the unacceptable in order to survive emotionally. But one experience shook me out of the almost matter-of-fact manner with which I had quickly learned to view such horrors. I watched a little boy die. His mother was sitting rocking him, trying to comfort him with her singsong moanings when, suddenly, he just stopped breathing. His frail frame, with the dried-out skin stretched over its bones, went limp in his mother's arms. Her moans turned into screaming and wailing. And it all happened while I watched.

Those who know me would expect me to start my discussion on Christianity and wealth with a story like that one. I can just hear some of the more cynical among them saying, "There he goes again—using guilt manipulation in order to get us to give some of our money to feed the poor."

I cannot say that those who criticize me in this regard are wrong. If attempting to bring people under conviction so that repentance may follow their acknowledgment of guilt, then I stand ready to be accused. If making some rich Christians feel distressed because they have adopted an affluent lifestyle of conspicuous wealth while turning their backs upon the desperately poor of the world is guilt manipulation, then I must acknowledge that I am guilty of it. Guilt, I believe, is a proper reaction to sin. And I believe that there *is* something sinful about some of us Christians buying piles of stuff we do not need, use, or for that matter particularly enjoy, while we ignore people whose basic needs go unmet. The apostle John properly asks,

> But whoso hath this world's good, and seeth his brother have need, and shutteth up his bowels of compassion from him, how dwelleth the love of God in him? My little children, let us not love in word, neither in tongue; but in deed and in truth (1 John 3:17–18).

In December of 1987, I had the wonderful opportunity of speaking at the great Urbana missionary conference sponsored by Inter-Varsity Christian Fellowship. In the course of my address to the more than eighteen thousand collegians who had gathered for that historic conclave, I asked a rather rhetorical question, "Can a Christian own a BMW?"

I had prefaced my question by telling those young people that Christians are people who do what Jesus would do if Jesus were in their place and facing their choices or options. I had gone on to point out that if Jesus lived in our contemporary world, like each of us He probably would have to buy a car. But I argued that if He had an extra thirty-five thousand dollars in His hand, I did not think He would spend it all on a luxury car, knowing that people in some Third World countries were starving to death. I contended that Jesus would probably buy a reliable but reasonably priced car and find some way to use the rest of that money to help those needy people.

The students who were there at the conference greeted my claims with approving applause. Unfortunately for me, some of their pastors and parents back home were not so enthusiastic. Over the next few months, I received several tempered and reasonable letters challenging my remarks.

It was not and is not my main intention to put BMW owners on a guilt trip. Nor is it my intention to allow the rest of us, who find other means to be extravagant, to escape feeling guilty. I am using the BMW as a symbol of the kind of spending into which all of us are being lured by our consumer-oriented society.

American economist Thorsten Veblen uses the phrase "conspicuous consumption" to suggest that certain items, including luxury automobiles, are often purchased more to make a statement as to who the owner thinks he or she is than to fulfill a need or even a *real* want. Christians, along with the rest of society, are being manipulated into gratifying *artificially* created wants while ignoring the basic needs of the wretched of the world.

Young people know this, and so do those of us who are not so young. But the general idea of it is easier to live with than the discomfort created when a single item, like the BMW, is mentioned. Perhaps the last question I should have asked those young people at Urbana is, "What is *your* BMW?" It may not be something that you drive, but you need to know what it is.

Some who hear this analysis and conclusion about what following Jesus means in today's world will ask, "Where do you draw the line? If buying a BMW is wrong, cannot the same argument be made for buying a new Ford? Why not an old Ford instead of a new one? If buying a Brooks Brothers suit is wrong, do we not have to raise questions about anything less than a cheap suit bought at the Salvation Army Thrift Store?"

The apostle Paul tells us that the children of God are people whose activities and decisions in everyday life are to be guided by the Holy Spirit: "For as many as are led by the Spirit of God, they are the sons of God" (Rom. 8:14). That means that each of us should endeavor to obey the will of God insofar as we can discern that will through Scripture, our shared reflections with fellow Christians, and those inner impulses which we sense are from God Himself.

Unfortunately, most of us are not so much led by these divine inspirations as we are by ads on television and the consumption styles dictated by the dominant culture. What we buy is much more under the control of the media than under the lordship of Christ. To be Christian involves having a Christlike spending pattern that is ordered by God.

In our present-day culture, we have coined the term "yuppie" for those who are young, upwardly mobile professionals. Even a cursory study of those who fit this definition reveals the majority of them to be people with little social concern, few emotional loyalties, and a hard-nosed concern for "the bottom line" in all of life's affairs. The epitome of this lifestyle has been emblazoned on a sweatshirt which reads, "The one who dies with the most toys wins." One cannot espouse that philosophy and conform to the description of the kind of people Jesus told us to be when He said,

> Therefore I say unto you, Take no thought for your life, what ye shall eat, or what ye shall drink; nor yet for your body, what ye shall put on. Is not the life more than meat, and the body than raiment? (Matt. 6:25).

Some who hear this analysis and conclusion about what following Jesus means in today's world will accuse me of being a killjoy and tell me that I am like Judas, who condemned *any* lavish expenditures when the money could be used to feed the poor (John 12:3–8). These critics contend that I leave no room in life for using wealth for celebration. This line of argument has always troubled me—especially the bit that compares my own attitude, with some accuracy, to that of the man who betrayed Christ. (Please note, however, that the writers of the Gospels acknowledge that the real sin in Judas' remarks lay in the fact that he was really a thief and was not intending to give the money to the poor at all!)

My comeback to these criticisms is derived from the biblical perspective on tithing as outlined in Deuteronomy 14:22–27. A careful reading of that passage will reveal that what Moses was giving us in his instructions about tithing were guidelines on how much of our wealth should be spent for celebration, rather than how much should be set aside for the poor and needy.

Through Moses, the Lord dictated to the people of Israel that each year at the Passover feast they should bring to Jerusalem one-tenth of their assets. Please note that the tithe was not one-tenth of one's income (after taxes, according to some exponents), but one tenth of all that one owned. That means that the faithful Jew took stock of all of his possessions and then designated one-tenth of his total worth for his Passover gift. When this money was brought to Jerusalem for the Passover feast, it was not used for some noble charity or to support a missionary program. Instead, it was blown on a party. That's right—a party! There was singing and dancing (as a Baptist, I had to think twice about including that fact). There was the kind of bash that could be compared to what we Americans tried to pull off on our Fourth of July Bicentennial celebration.

Among the purposes for this celebration was to give the people of Israel a small foretaste of what the kingdom of God would be like when God sent His Son to establish it here on earth as it is in heaven. It was a sign that the future kingdom would be a party and not a soup kitchen. In the midst of the celebration, one could make the declaration, "You think this is something? Just you wait 'til the kingdom comes!"

Can you imagine the Jews in the ancient world blowing one-tenth of all of their assets on a party? No wonder the children of Israel said, "I was glad when they said unto me, let us go into the house of the Lord!" The celebration at Jerusalem was evidence of the kind of God we have. He is a party deity. The somber people of the world are going to have to do some adjusting if they are to be part of His kingdom. Jesus said as much when some of the drab religionists of His day complained that He was too much into partying:

> And saying, We have piped unto you, and ye have not danced; we have mourned unto you, and ye have not lamented. For John came neither eating nor drinking, and they say, He hath a devil. The Son of man came eating and drinking, and they say, Behold a man gluttonous, and a winebibber, a friend of publicans and sinners. But wisdom is justified of her children (Matt. 11:17–19).

The point here is that the biblical principle of tithing is a prescription for celebration rather than for charity. It tells us how much is ordained for partying rather than how much we are supposed to give to the poor. If Christians are filled with the love of God, they are likely to end up like St. Francis of Assisi—giving away *everything* and leaving nothing for their own pleasure. It seems to me that God has put some limitations on our giving so that we might enjoy something of His future for us in the present. In short, tithing seems to suggest one-tenth for the party and the other nine-tenths to be used with careful scrutiny as to ways it can bless others, particularly the poor of the world.

It is interesting to recognize that even in celebration we must be mindful of the unfortunate of the world. At the banquets of the godly, the poor and downtrodden must be honored guests. Those whom the world has rejected must be invited:

> Go ye therefore into the highways, and as many as ye shall find, bid to the marriage. So those servants went out into the highways, and gathered together all as many as they found, both bad and good: and the wedding was furnished with guests (Matt. 22:9–10).

When I pick up this theme of what we should do with wealth, I am dealing with a major theme of Scripture. There are over six hundred references and declarations in Scripture pertaining to our use of money. In the New Testament, especially, the references are everywhere; for instance, in the Epistle of James, one out of every five verses deals with this theme. Jesus makes responding to the needs of the poor the criteria for evaluation when we all stand before the Eternal Judge of history (Matt. 25:31–46). There are many prophetic voices in our time who remind us that Jesus so identifies with the poor and oppressed of the world that those who want to love Him would do well to look for Him among these "least of the brethren."

Perhaps the most striking message on what rich people are supposed to do with their wealth comes to us in the words of Jesus to the rich young ruler:

> And when he was gone forth into the way, there came one running, and kneeled to him, and asked him, Good Master, what shall I do that I may inherit eternal life? And Jesus said unto him, Why callest thou me good? there is none good but one, that is, God. Thou knowest the commandments, Do not commit adultery, Do not kill, Do not steal, Do not bear false witness, Defraud not, Honour thy father and mother. And he answered and said unto him, Master, all these have I observed from my youth. Then Jesus beholding him loved him, and said unto him, One thing thou lackest: go thy way, sell whatsoever thou hast, and give to the poor, and thou shalt have treasure in heaven: and come, take up the cross, and follow me. And he was sad at that saying, and went away grieved: for he had great possessions (Mark 10:17–22).

Although salvation does not come from good works (see Eph. 2:8–9), there is no question that wealth is a barrier to having the faith that saves. Rich people (and that includes most of us in the United States, who are wealthy by international standards) are afraid of getting too much into Jesus because they sense that it will cost them—and indeed it will. The wealthy are threatened by the call of Christ, who bids us to leave all and die for him. They have too much to lose. The rich know that if they take the biblical Jesus seriously, they will have to do more than get their priorities right, which is what some preachers who are afraid to disturb the socioeconomic order in their congregations suggest was all that Jesus meant to say to the rich young ruler. We, the wealthy Christians of the world, know all too well that Jesus calls us to abandon the things of this world, use our resources to feed the poor, and take up a cross.

Whenever I start talking about the Christian responsibility to respond to the needs of the poor, there are some church leaders who get very upset. I cannot tell you how many times pastors have invited me to lead evangelistic services in their churches, only to tell me nervously at the last minute not to say anything that might adversely affect the giving of their congregation to the building fund. There is ample awareness among these pastors that if people truly have their hearts touched by the needs of the poor, they will be less inclined to give sacrificially for new stained-glass windows and sanctuaries. And of course, they are right. But a church that is more interested in providing for itself than in giving itself in service to a needy world is not the kind of church which our Lord had in mind on the day of Pentecost. There is something wrong with an ecclesiastical hierarchy which designates billions to build structures to honor One who said that He did not dwell in buildings made with hands. I am not convinced that God is all that honored by a church that puts up buildings for His glory while sacrificing comparatively little for those who cannot escape from grinding poverty.

In ancient Israel there was reason to build a glorious temple—God was mysteriously present in the Holy of Holies of the sanctuary on Mount Zion. But all of that changed with the death and resurrection of Christ. When He was on the cross, the veil of the temple was rent in twain and the special presence of God which had been radiantly present there came bursting out. Since the Holy Spirit has come upon us, that special presence is now in all of us who are His temples (see Acts 17:24 and 1 Cor. 3:17).

When I plead on behalf of the poor I am not against using some resources for art. Man shall not live by bread alone, and limiting spending to utilitarian purposes is not a requirement for the Christian lifestyle. Obviously, basic needs must be met first, but all of us have a God-given hunger for that which is beautiful. People—especially poor people whose lives tend to be very drab—need beauty for their souls.

Some Roman Catholic missionaries in Haiti made a herculean effort to get together enough money to build a concert hall and establish a symphony orchestra in the city of Port-au-Prince. There were some who criticized their work and argued that it was crazy to provide concerts for starving people. I, myself, had serious doubts as to the wisdom of the project until opening night. Those who saw the faces of the ragged people who jammed that concert hall to hear the symphony were left with no doubt that the money had been used wisely. There was something mystically beautiful being taken in by these poverty-beaten people. There was something given to them that evening that made life a little more bearable. There was something that happened under the spell of the music that made people who had been hardened by need into softer, kinder folk. Everyone at the concert could feel God at work, providing something precious for the poor.

My concern about art is that it has become far too expensive, and hence far too elitist, to serve humanity as God intended it to do. The high prices of theater tickets and concert tickets exclude too many from the blessings which art can provide. When even art museums cost several dollars to get in, some gifts from God are denied to many people who already have too little beauty in their lives.

If students of the arts come to me and ask me if they can serve God as musicians, actors, painters, or dancers, I always answer, "Of course!" But then I go on to tell them they must make their talents a gift to all people, not just those who can afford expensive tickets. We need art for all the people. We need plays and music on street corners and parks, and great art in public buildings so that everyone can enjoy it. We must educate people to appreciate art so that they can respect it and enjoy it. Insofar as art enriches, sensitizes, and makes people more human, it can be viewed as a gift of God, and those who deliver such a gift to people who need it truly are servants of God. Art need not be extravagant to be good. It need not be expensive to be a precious gift. And it can be legitimate for a church to spend money on art. Enriching the lives of others through art and music can be a good gift which the church can give to the world. Unfortunately, much of what is spent by churches for facilities is neither artistic nor necessary.

Finally, please let it be known that I am by no means attacking the production of wealth. With John Wesley, I strongly urge everyone to "work as hard as you can, to make all the money you can, and spend as little as you can in order to give away all that you can."

I do not think it is a sin to make a million dollars, but it can become a sin not to spend that million dollars as Jesus would if He were in your place. Undoubtedly, we all sin in our spending behavior, but the fact that none of us does things just like Christ would is no reason to throw up our hands and give up. Each and every day, we who have not attained a Christlike style of spending should be pressing to become more like Jesus in all that we do:

> Brethren, I count not myself to have apprehended: but this one thing I do, forgetting those things which are behind, and reaching forth unto those things which are before, I press toward the mark for the prize of the high calling of God in Christ Jesus (Phil. 3:13–14).

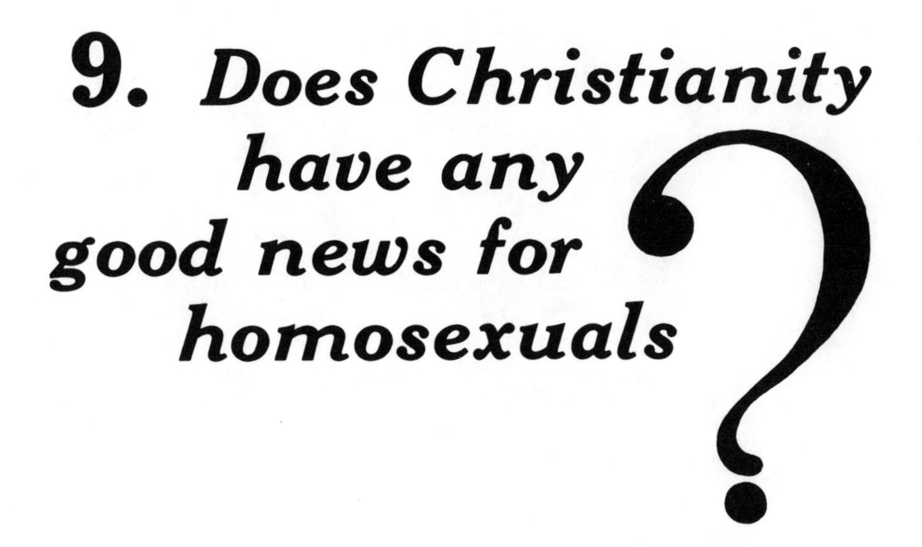

9. *Does Christianity have any good news for homosexuals?*

I HAVE A FRIEND who is a pastor in Brooklyn and who is one of the most sensitive and loving men I know. He pastors a church that has seen better days. The community around the church has undergone great change, so that many of the old church members have moved away and very few new people have come in to take their places. It is a church that is struggling to stay alive.

The people of this church love my friend and try to do as well by him financially as they are able, but he still has a hard time economically. Fortunately, he is helped out by the local undertakers, who often call him to do funerals nobody else will do. When people who have no church affiliations die, somebody has to do their funerals, and my friend is one of those somebodies.

From time to time, I call this man to find out what is going on in his life. Because he serves in the place where he does, all kinds of strange and unusual things happen to him. His experiences have proven to be an invaluable source of illustrations for my books and sermons.

One day as we were talking, I asked him if anything special had happened to him in the past week. He could not think of anything, so I helped him out by getting more specific. "What did you do last Tuesday morning at ten o'clock?" I inquired.

"Oh! That was an interesting morning," he responded.

"What happened to make it so interesting?" I asked.

"Well," he said, "I got a call that morning from the undertaker who has his place just down the street. He needed somebody to do a funeral and nobody else he called wanted anything to do with this one because the man had died of AIDS. Since he couldn't get anybody else, I told him I'd take the funeral."

"What was it like?" I inquired.

"It was strange," he answered. "When I got to the funeral home, I found about twenty-five or thirty homosexual men waiting for me. They were in the room with the casket, just sitting as though they were frozen in their chairs. They looked as though they were statues. Each of them faced straight ahead with glassy, unfocused eyes. Their hands were folded on their laps as though some teacher had ordered them to sit that way. They almost scared me. Several of them wore the kind of clothes that made a blatant statement about who and what they were.

"I did what I was supposed to do," my friend said. "I read some Scripture and said some prayers. I made the kind of remarks that ministers are supposed to make when they really don't know the dead person. After a few minutes, I ended the service and prepared to go out to the cemetery. Then I, along with those men, got into the cars that were to follow the hearse. We rode through the Holland Tunnel to the cemetery which was located near Hoboken, New Jersey. Then we all got out of the cars and went over to the edge of the grave.

"Not a word was spoken by any of those men from the beginning of the funeral until I had finished the prayers to commit the remains of the dead man to the earth. They all just stood at the edge of the grave, as motionless as they had been when they were seated in the funeral home. I said the closing prayer and the benediction, and turned to leave. Then, I realized that all of those men were still standing frozen in their places, all with blank expressions on their faces. I turned and walked back to them and asked if there was anything more I could do for them. One of them spoke."

"What did he say?" I asked.

"What he said surprised me," my friend answered. "He asked me to read the Twenty-third Psalm. He said, 'When I got up this morning to come to this funeral, I was looking forward to somebody reading the Twenty-third Psalm to me. I really like that psalm, and I figured that they always read the Twenty-third Psalm at funerals. You didn't read the Twenty-third Psalm.'

"I read the Twenty-third Psalm for those men," my friend said. "When I finished, a second man spoke, and he asked me to read another passage of Scripture. He wanted to hear that part of the Bible where it says that there is *nothing* that can separate us from the love of God. So I read from the eighth chapter of Romans where Paul tells us that neither death nor life, nor angels, nor principalities, nor powers, nor things present, nor things to come, nor height, nor depth, nor any other creature shall be able to separate us from the love of God, which is in Christ Jesus.

"When I read to those men that *nothing* could separate them from the love of God, I saw some signs of emotion on their faces for the first time. Then, one after the other, they made special requests for me to read favorite passages of Scripture. I stood there for almost an hour reading Scripture to those homosexual men before we went to our cars and headed back to Brooklyn."

When I heard that story, I almost cried. Something down deep inside of me hurt. Something in my heart ached with sadness. I realized that these men my friend described were hungry for the Word of God but would never set foot inside a church. They wanted to hear the Bible, but they wanted to stay clear of Christians, and I think I know why. I think they feel that Christians despise them. And they are probably right.

Oh, I know there are exceptions, and here and there we can find church people who have overcome their homophobia (fear of homosexuals) and have reached out to the gay community with Christian love, but they are few and far between. For the most part, the reaction of Christian people to homosexuals has been unmitigated horror and disgust. Few things have generated as much animosity and anger among evangelicals as have the homosexuals in churches who have dared to "come out of the closet" and tell the household of faith who and what they are.

I am *not* asking that Christian people gloss over biblical teachings or ignore their conviction that homosexual acts are sin. I am not asking that we make a case to justify homosexual behavior. I am simply reminding Christian people that we are supposed to love people—even those people who offend us. I am calling on Christians to reach out and show kindness and affection toward their homosexual neighbors. (There are at least fifteen million such neighbors in the United States.) If we Christians cannot love these neighbors as we love ourselves, then we are violating the command of Jesus (Matt. 19:19) and ought to cease calling ourselves His followers. Loving people is more than trying to generate some mushy sentimental emotions. Loving is a commitment to treating people as Jesus would treat them if He were in our places.

Love requires justice. I believe that if Jesus were in our shoes, He would reach out in love to His homosexual brothers and sisters, and His love would be translated into a call for them to be justly treated by others. That call for justice would require that we work to end the discrimination that has made homosexuals into second-class citizens and denied them their constitutional rights. His love would lead Him to work to create an atmosphere in society wherein homosexuals could be open about who they are and no longer live in fear of oppression and persecution. That does not mean that gay people should have the right to insist that the rest of society consider homosexual behavior to be simply another different, but normal, lifestyle. It does mean that those people who have a homosexual orientation should be treated as human beings who have dignity.

It is *very* important that all of us distinguish between homosexual *orientation* and homosexual *behavior.* Homosexual orientation is an inclination to desire sexual intimacy with members of the same sex. Homosexual behavior is "making love" or seeking sexual gratification through physical interaction with members of the same sex. The first is desire. The second is action. The first is temptation. The second is yielding to temptation.

I personally know many Christians with a homosexual orientation who fight against their desire for homosexual behavior through the power of the Holy Spirit. The desire to have sexual gratification through physical involvement with persons of their own sex is a constant (just as heterosexual desire can be a constant for many) with many of them, but they are "more than conquerors through Christ who strengtheneth" them (Rom. 8:37).

I cannot help but admire these brave saints who endure lives of sexual frustration because of their commitment to what they believe are biblical admonitions against homosexual intercourse. Many such Christians have told me about their long nights of spiritual agony as they have struggled against the flesh to remain faithful to what they believe to be the will of God. Any who believe that these homosexuals who remain celibate for the sake of Christ are anything less than glorious victors in God's kingdom ought to be ashamed of themselves.

There are those who say that victory over temptation is not enough for a homosexual to be a Christian. They argue that to be saved, homosexuals must also be free from their homosexual orientation. In short, these people think that homosexuals should be transformed into heterosexuals through prayer. They back up their argument with examples of people whom they have heard about who have been "healed" of homosexuality and are now leading happy heterosexual lives. They say that what God has done for these "former" homosexuals, He can and will do for anyone who asks Him.

I do not argue with the claim that God *can* do anything. After all, God is God. But there is a big difference between saying what God *can* do and what He *will* do. The former is a doctrine; the latter is a presumption. The "name it—claim it" types upset me with their overly simplistic approach to this complicated problem. Just because God *can* do something does not mean that He *will*—even if we beg Him to do so.

If that sounds like heresy, read it again carefully. I know too many people who have prayed desperately for something God can do, only to find that for reasons incomprehensible to us, He does not.

People such as Dietrich Bonhoffer, the Christian martyr, who prayed for the deliverance of the Jews during the Holocaust, discovered that the God who could deliver them did not. How many Christians have prayed for a loved one to be delivered from cancer, only to have the loved one die? They prayed to a God who *could* heal cancer and who *has* healed cancer in many, many other cases, but who did *not* heal the special person for whom they prayed. And I know homosexuals who have prayed desperately and to exhaustion to be delivered from their homosexual orientation without the result for which they yearned.

Yes, I believe that *all* prayers are eventually answered. Some of them will be answered in heaven. But we live in the ugly here-and-now rather than the sweet by-and-by, and a lot of evangelical homosexuals are suffering frustration in spite of their earnest prayers. I do not understand why this is so, but I cannot deny that it is so.

I know of one case wherein the simplistic theory of deliverance expounded by a sincere but naïve preacher drove a young man to suicide. The preacher had told him that if he were a Christian whom God loved, then God would answer his prayers for deliverance and turn him into a heterosexual. The young man prayed long and hard to no avail. He concluded that if Christians whom God loves were delivered from their homosexual orientations, then he must not be a Christian whom God loved. In accord with some interpretations he had heard of Romans 1:26–27, he was sure that his past sins had caused God to give up on him. His despair and despondency over his supposed state of rejection by God led him one dismal afternoon to blow his brains out.

I think that many of the despicable attitudes toward homosexuals stem from an ignorance of what science is discovering, as well as a lack of understanding as to what the Bible says. First of all, there is a growing body of evidence that suggests that most homosexuals have the orientation that they do through no choice of their own nor any failure on the part of their parents to socialize them properly. More and more research suggests that in a great number of cases, if not in an overwhelming majority, homosexual orientation is inborn.

I knew before I made it that such a statement would incur the wrath of many of my evangelical friends. So I double-checked my facts to make sure my information was up-to-date. I called my colleague, William M. Kephart, who for years served as professor of sociology at the University of Pennsylvania. He was the first to introduce me to this perspective, and I wanted to find out if he was still convinced of it. Kephart let me know in no uncertain terms that for most people who are homosexuals, biological factors are the cause.

I then went to the empirical research presently being done by physiologists. Much as I expected, the most up-to-date findings confirm that *in animals* (and it is important to recognize that humans are different from and more than animals), sexual orientation is controlled by biological factors—specifically by hormones. Research done by many scientists (see the bibliography at the end of this chapter) shows that when there is a disruption of certain hormones at a crucial stage in the development of the fetus, the sexual orientation of rats can be significantly altered. Such a disruption might be caused by some trauma or intense nervous tension in the mother during her pregnancy. The research suggests that sexual orientation is the result of programming or "imprinting" the brain of the rat fetus, and that the upset experienced by the mother can mess up this process, resulting in the homosexual orientation of her offspring.

When we come to humans, it is difficult if not impossible to get the kind of evidence we need to make assertions one way or the other about the influence of biological factors on homosexual orientations. Some important research on the influence of hormones on human sexual orientation has been done by John Money of Johns Hopkins University. His limited findings raise doubts about sexual orientation's being the result of prenatal conditioning of the brain. But he does not discount hormonal factors completely. As a matter of fact, Money suggests that *socialization,* rather than prenatal tensions, may influence the hormonal programming of the brain, with the result being significant alteration of the sexual orientation. Thus, even Money allows that biological factors may control whether or not persons become homosexuals. (For other studies on humans, see the bibliography at the end of this chapter.)

The reason I have taken this limited excursion into the empirical research on the origins of sexual orientation is obvious. If many of those who have a homosexual orientation are the way they are through no fault of their own, but rather as a result of inborn conditions or hormonal changes, then it becomes dubious that much can be accomplished simply by asking such persons to repent and choose to be heterosexuals. In my opinion, homosexuals are the way they are because all of nature is fallen or out of whack. I personally believe that all homo sapiens were meant to be heterosexual. But that does not change the fact that in this fallen world, the orientation of many homosexuals is natural (that is, the result of natural biological factors).

I am not suggesting that *all* homosexual orientation is the result of hormonal factors. Actually, I believe that there may be a variety of causes for this orientation, including problems in the socialization of the young and faulty parental identification. What I do claim is that most homosexuals did not consciously *choose* their orientation.

In Romans 1 we read,

> For this cause God gave them up unto vile affections: for even their women did change the natural use into that which is against nature: And likewise also the men, leaving the natural use of the woman, burned in their lust one toward another; men with men working that which is unseemly, and receiving in themselves that recompence of their error which was meet (Rom. 1:26–27).

There are many who argue that this passage does not condemn those with homosexual orientations. They say rather that it condemns those whose natural desires are heterosexual but who, by giving unrestrained vent to their lusts, become debased and decadent. They contend that Paul is condemning those who *choose* to get into homosexual behavior as a means to get new or "kinky" sexual thrills. Some homosexuals I know believe that this passage refers to heterosexuals who adopt homosexuality as perversion rather than to those who are born with a homosexual orientation.

I think there may be some validity to this argument but personally I hold to a belief that homosexual *behavior* is wrong, regardless of what motivates it. I hold to this position not only because I disagree with my homosexual friends about this particular scripture, but also because for centuries the consensus of church leaders and theologians has been that homosexual behavior is against the will of God. I believe that our contemporary reading of Scripture should be informed by the traditions of Christendom. The traditional interpretations of Scripture should not be considered infallible (else there would have been no Protestant Reformation) but they should be taken seriously.

In addition to what Paul writes in this passage in Romans, he makes a couple of other references:

> Know ye not that the unrighteous shall not inherit the kingdom of God? Be not deceived: neither fornicators, nor idolaters, nor adulterers, nor effeminate, nor abusers of themselves with mankind (1 Cor. 6:9).

> For whoremongers, for them that defile themselves with mankind, for menstealers, for liars, for perjured persons, and if there be any other thing that is contrary to sound doctrine (1 Tim. 1:10).

But even here there are words of caution for those who would make too easy an application of Scripture to condemn contemporary homosexual behavior.

Among some of the most respected biblical scholars (see Robin Scroggs, *The New Testament and Homosexuality*), there is wide acceptance of the opinion that in these passages, Paul was condemning the ancient Greek practice of pederasty. In ancient Greece, much education took place on an individual basis. A given teacher would take on a particular young boy and personally tutor him. In this close relationship of teacher and pupil, it was not uncommon for the teacher to exploit his position of power over his student and either seduce his student or force him to enter into intimate sexual relations with him.

These young boys were considered to be desirable sexual objects only in their early adolescence. With the growth of a beard and the appearance of the other physical changes that go along with maturation, the young student would lose his sexual attractiveness. This was because the Greek culture had established the youthful boy as its most erotic sexual object. (On this basis, many have contended that the culture of ancient Greece was "sick.") When the student was no longer desirable to the teacher, he usually was cast aside for newer and younger sexual partners.

Those who were thus abandoned were usually left psychologically devastated and often suicidal. Many students tried to prolong their boyish attractiveness by concealing their oncoming maturity. Taking on effeminate mannerisms was one such technique employed by these psychologically and physically abused young men.

This practice of pederasty was abhorrent to the apostle Paul. He took great offense at all forms of sexual exploitation, and this hideous form, so common in ancient Greece, was particularly a target of his ire. To compare pederasty to a relationship chosen in love is considered by Scroggs and by other biblical ethicists to be a serious mistake.

Please remember that I *do* think that homosexual behavior is contrary to the will of God. But I do *not* think the Scripture should be made to speak in ways which are not in accord with how it was intended to speak in order to make my case. It is too easy for any of us out of intense emotion to use Scripture in inexact ways to affirm what we believe to be right or to condemn what we believe to be wrong.

While there is no doubt in my mind that homosexual behavior has always been unacceptable to Christians, I find it interesting to note that the New Testament does not give as much space or attention to this sin as it does to others, such as neglect of the poor or lack of love for others. Actually, Jesus never alludes to homosexuality in His teachings. The fact that homosexuality has become such an overriding concern for many contemporary preachers may be more a reflection of the homophobia of the church than it is the result of the emphasis of Scripture.

In this discussion, I have primarily concentrated on the homosexual problem as it pertains to men. It is not that I am unaware of the fact that homosexuality also occurs among females (although according to most surveys, male homosexuals outnumber female homosexuals at least four to one), but rather that the research about the origins of female homosexual orientation is, so far as I can ascertain, much more confusing and ambiguous than the research done on the origins of male homosexuality. Among women, there is much more evidence of sociological/psychological causes of this condition. For instance, there are large numbers of cases wherein the homosexual orientation may be a reaction to being sexually abused, particularly by fathers.

In short, I do not have much to say on the issue of female homosexuality, in part because there is even less known about it than there is about male homosexuality. However, once again I reaffirm my belief that to claim that the causal factors of all homosexual orientations are the same is wrong. And once again, I believe that the case may be made that biological conditions rather than sociological/psychological conditions are primary contributors to generating a homosexual orientation in many instances.

I am by no means arguing that we should discount the possibility that in some cases people are into the homosexual lifestyle because they have been seduced into it or because they chose to be into it. Because sin still abounds in both the heterosexual and homosexual worlds, a lot of people are hurt and confused. However, I do believe that a great proportion of both males and females who are homosexual in their orientation did not choose to be this way, and a significant number of them who desperately want to get out of this orientation are finding little hope or help from either science or religion.

Very often evangelical homosexuals find themselves incredibly torn, not only between their basic sexual orientation and what they believe is taught by the Word of God, but also between life in the homosexual community, which seems to hold some promise of acceptance and companionship, and life in the "straight" world, which may be filled with estrangement and loneliness. Undoubtedly there are some evangelical homosexuals who choose to live in the homosexual community because they see no alternative to living out life alone if they choose to remain celibate Christians and to take their places among the rest of us. Their agonies over the prospects of loneliness are seldom appreciated by those of us who do not have to face the problem. We, who would be sensitive to the needs of homosexuals, must be looking for some creative answers to this dilemma.

Recently two homosexual men who live in Chicago solved their problem of loneliness by establishing a covenant wherein they promised to live with each other "til death do them part," even though they simultaneously pledged to remain celibate. They chose to live together as lifelong partners "in all love and tenderness" but without any sexual intercourse going between them. These two men claimed to be enjoying the humanizing benefits of a genuine love relationship that has provided them with mutual blessings but did not violate biblical admonitions to refrain from homosexual intercourse. Over the past year I have learned of a number of other homosexual couples who are evangelicals and have adopted a similar arrangement.

I choose to call this a homosexual "covenant" rather than a homosexual "marriage." I refrain from using the word *marriage* because I think that implies a sexually consummated relationship. On the other hand, the word covenant connotes a lifelong commitment of mutual obligation which does not necessitate sexual intercourse.

There are Christians who will disapprove of this arrangement, claiming that the Bible implies a condemnation of even romantic feelings between members of the same sex. However, these critics are hard-pressed to build a biblical case for their complaints. If they say that lovers cannot live in such a relationship without becoming sexually involved, they are making a value judgment about the moral strength and integrity of other Christians. Their judgments may be more the result of psychological projection than what has in reality been proven to be true. While I realize that many will consider me naïve to believe that such an arrangement could work, I do think it is possible.

Those of us evangelicals who regularly are asked for counsel by homosexuals find ourselves in difficult situations. On the one hand, our obedience to the teachings of the Bible and the traditions of the church necessitates that we withhold approval of homosexual intercourse. Even if the New Testament case against homosexual intercourse is not as pronounced as some people think it is, there are still passages in the Old Testament that speak directly to the issue which I find impossible to dismiss (see Lev. 18:22, 20:13). On the other hand, we are hard-pressed to find any biblical basis for condemning deep love commitments between homosexual Christians, as long as those commitments are not expressed in sexual intercourse.

Perhaps an even better answer to the threat of loneliness faced by homosexuals is to live in the context of a Christian community. Thousands of Christians across America are finding that it is beneficial both spiritually and economically to live together in groups ranging from three or four to ten or more (see also chapter 13). These Christian communities can foster a high level of commitment among the members. In these larger social units, the temptation to consummate sexual urges on the part of a homosexual person could be held in check by the loving and prayerful support of others. A setting would be created where the homosexual person felt safe being honest about his or her orientation, and the others in the group could make special efforts to encourage a lifestyle that glorifies Christ.

In such a community, there would be times when the person with a homosexual orientation would be able to use his or her own gifts from God to help the other members, being able to set aside for a time the "issue" of being homosexual. And if small communities were able to be open about including persons with both homosexual and heterosexual orientations, the larger evangelical community would be challenged to realize that "they" are indeed part of "us" and that we are to be mutually responsible and compassionate.

Persons with a homosexual orientation should not be forced to discover and use the gifts they have for the body of Christ exclusively in the context of homosexuality, unless that is where they feel called, any more than an alcoholic should be relegated to working and interacting only with other alcoholics. Some of our homosexual brothers and sisters have, through their struggles, grown in the Lord to the point where they have wisdom that would benefit and bless the rest of us.

To make myself perfectly clear, of course I am not saying that homosexuals should engage in homosexual sex in or out of the community. Just as an alcoholic should not drink, none of us should act in ways unbecoming to the gospel of Christ. But the church—and all of our local churches—loses when we see people as stereotypes and labels rather than as our brothers and sisters in Christ.

There *must* be good news for homosexuals. In the likelihood that most of them will still have their basic sexual orientations regardless of their efforts to change, we must do more than simply bid them be celibate. We must find ways for them to have fulfilling, loving experiences so that they might have their humanity affirmed and their incorporation into the Body of Christ insured. Homosexuals *are* our brothers and sisters and must be treated that way. To do less is sin.

Sex differentiation bibliography

I. Reports on biological/physical factors influencing sexual orientation in animals.

Hoepfner. (1988) "Prenatal and Neonatal Androgen Exposure Interact to Affect Sex Differentiation in Female Rats." *Behavioral Neuroscience,* 102:61.

Tonjes. (1977) "Neonatal Intracerebral Sex Steroid on Sexual Behavior, Play Behavior and Gonad." *Experimental and Clinical Endocrinology,* 90:257.

Dejonse. (1988) "Sex Behavior and Sex Orientation in Female Rats." *Hormones and Behavior,* 22:100.

Harris, G. W., and Levine, S. (1962) "Sexual Differentiation of the Brain and Its Experimental Control." *Journal of Physiology,* 163:42–44.

Beach, F. A. (1976) "Sexual Attractivity, Proceptivity, and Receptivity in Female Mammals." *Hormones and Behavior,* 7:105–138.

Pfaff, D. W., and Zigmond, R. E. (1971) "Neonatal Androgen Effects on Sexual and Non-sexual Behavior of Adult Rats Tested under Various Hormone Regimes." *Neuroendrocrinology,* 7:129–145.

II. Primate Studies.

Goy, R. W. (1970) "Experimental Control of Psychosexuality." *Philosophical Transactions of the Royal Society of London Series B: Biological Sciences,* 259:149–162.

Phoenix, D. H., Jensen, J. N., and Chamber, K. C. (1983) "Female Sexual Behavior Displayed by Androgenized

Female Rhesus Macaques." *Hormones and Behavior,* 17:146–151.

III. Reports on biological/physical factors influencing sexual orientation in humans.

Money, J., Schwartz, M., and Lewis, V. G. (1984) "Adult Erotosexual Status and Fetal Hormonal Masculinization and Demasculinization: 46, XX Congenital Virilizing Adrenal Hyperplasia and 46, XY Androgen-Insensitivity Syndrome Compared." *Psychoneuroendocrinology,* 9:405–414.

Money, J., and Ehrhardt, A. A. (1972) "Man and Woman, Boy and Girl." Baltimore: Johns Hopkins Press.

Money, J., Ehrhardt, A. A., and Mascia, D. N. (1968) "Fetal Feminization Induced by Androgen Insensitivity in the Testicular Feminizing Syndrome: Effect on Marriage and Maternalism." *The Johns Hopkins Medical Journal,* 123:105–114.

Ehrhardt, A. A., and Meyer-Bahlburg, H. F. L. (1981) "Effects of Prenatal Sex Hormones on Gender Related Behavior." *Science,* 211:1312–1318.

Imperato-McGinley, J., Peterson, R. E., Stoller, R., and Goodwin, W. E. (1979) "Male Pseudohermaphroditism Secondary to 17B-Hydroxysteroid Dehydrosenase Deficiency: Gender Role Change with Puberty." *Journal of Clinical Endocrinology and Metabolism,* 49:391–395.

Imperato-McGinley, J., Guerrero, L., Gautier, T., and Peterson, R. E. (1974) "Steroid 5 Alpha-Reductase Deficiency in Man: An Inherited Form of Male Pseudohermaphroditism." *Science,* 186:1213–1215.

IV. For a review of biblical and theological opinions on homosexuality, see:

Scroggs, Robin, *The New Testament and Homosexuality,* Fortress Press, 1983.

10. Should preachers start preaching against sports?

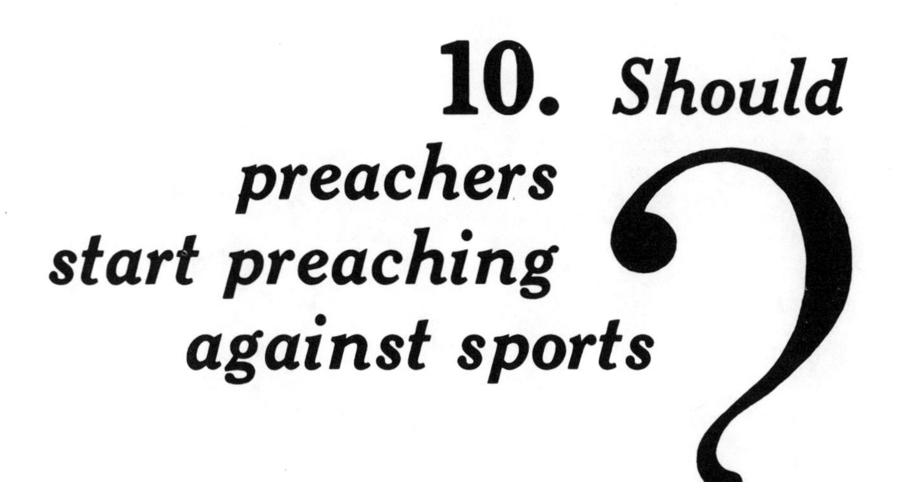

SPORTS HAVE ALWAYS been considered healthy for Christian young people. Those of us who were raised in fundamentalist piety were forbidden to dance or go to movies, but we were told that sports were wholesome and good. The church in which I grew up had a basketball team and a softball team, and we took the playing of sports very seriously—perhaps a bit too seriously.

Since my boyhood days, I have seen the steady growth of the role of sports in the Christian community. It has reached such a level of importance in some churches that the ministers know they must plan all church activities around the schedules of high-school ball games and must also be concerned lest the playoff games in professional sports keep people away from important meetings. There is evidence that sports may be getting out of hand. Some of us share a growing concern that sports not only have become a *threat* to religion, but in some respects may have *become* a religion.

Religion has been defined as that which ultimately concerns us and demands our utmost commitment. It is that which controls our behavior and conditions our capacity for joy or sorrow. As such, sports can rightly be called a religion for many people. For them it *is* their ultimate concern and elicits a commitment that makes what the church gets from them pale by comparison.

In 1980, the Soviet Union invaded Afghanistan. As a protest, President Jimmy Carter ordered the U.S. boycott of the Olympics, which that year were to be held in Moscow. This political statement caused incredible heartbreak for hundreds of athletes who for years had trained for the privilege and honor of participating in the Olympics. There were outcries that the American boycott had dashed lifetime hopes and dreams and even destroyed the meaning of life for many of the athletes.

One thoughtful Olympic athlete who was interviewed on television reflected on some positive effects that had come from the cancellation of American participation. He pointed out that for the previous five years, he had done nothing else but get ready for the Games. He confessed to having cut off friendships because they required time that he could not afford to take away from his training. He said he had done very little to develop himself intellectually during those five years because all his energies had been focused upon being physically fit. By his own admission, athletics had become a religion to him and had crowded out any time or attention that might have been given to God.

This young athlete went on to express a certain gratitude for the cancellation of the Olympics because it had driven him to an awareness of how transient athletic fame was and how foolish it was for him to have given so much of himself to something that could be taken away so abruptly. This unusually wise young man confessed that his attention to sports had verged on sinful idolatry, and he expressed relief that the cancellation had freed him from a psychological bondage to sports which had kept him from more important concerns.

I have seen the same idolatrous tendencies in college athletics. In large universities, athletes who participate in major sports often get very little education. Their coaches tend to steer them away from any challenging courses in order to ensure that they remain academically eligible. And practice takes all their time! Collegiate athletes are expected to attend daily practices that can last five to seven hours. There is simply no way that these athletes can have sufficient quality time for classes and studies.

For many athletes, their four years in college provide only the illusion of an education. Many graduate as functional illiterates after having been exploited by institutions of higher education that have little regard for them beyond how many points they score and how many ticket-buying fans they can lure through the gates.

I find the exploitation of college athletes particularly offensive when I see what is happening to black athletes. Working as I do among inner-city blacks, I find that many of these young people believe that sports is their ticket to a better life. Over and over again I hear them tell me that athletic scholarships are going to provide for their educations and give them a chance to improve themselves. It becomes difficult, if not impossible, to convince them otherwise. But if they do get sports scholarships, it is unlikely that they will get much in the way of an education.

There are too few coaches like Dean Smith, the basketball coach of the University of North Carolina, or Joe Paterno, the football coach of Penn State, who value the academic achievement of their athletes above what they may be able to accomplish on the playing field. Too many collegiate athletes, especially black young people, are valued by their schools primarily for their entertainment value. And even if they are granted academic degrees, they graduate with few skills that will help them earn a good livelihood if they are unable to go on to professional sports.

The fact that all of this happens without the preachers of our churches crying out in protest is hard for me to understand. Certainly there is sufficient biblical basis for an outcry against such abuses. For instance, the apostle Paul wrote to Timothy,

> But refuse profane and old wives' fables, and exercise thyself rather unto godliness. For bodily exercise profiteth little: but godliness is profitable unto all things, having promise of the life that now is, and of that which is to come (1 Tim. 4:7–8).

It is not that Paul was opposed to athletics. Quite to the contrary, Paul had a great appreciation for sports. He drew many of his sermonic illustrations from the athletic games of his day. But Paul was well aware that sports could consume the participants, leaving them with little time and energy for the more important activities of Christian living.

I am sad to say that Christian colleges are sometimes not much better. When I was a student in a Christian college thirty years ago, we were well aware of the fact that our teams could not compete against those secular colleges which put a great emphasis on sports. We did not try to compete in the NCAA. We were told that we were in school to prepare for Christian service and that sports were only for recreation. Sports scholarships were things that secular schools gave to athletes. The administrators at the college I attended thought that scholarships ought to be for more lofty purposes (i.e., to help young people who were planning to go into the ministry or to the mission field), and even then only on the basis of need.

Today, however, Christian colleges have athletic programs that mirror those of the secular schools. Furthermore, the same exploitation of black athletes is taking place in Christian schools as we might find anywhere else. In many Christian colleges I visit, the only black students on campus are those on the ball teams.

That frightens me because, while I believe that there should be affirmative action to get minority students on Christian campuses, I do not believe that sports should be the instrument for recruitment and scholarships. There are many other contributions which minority students can make to campus life, and to limit our recognition of what they can offer us to athletics may be one of the most racist statements we can make. Certainly Christian colleges ought to do better, and their administrators ought to know better.

Each year I get to visit twenty to thirty different Christian college campuses. During those visits I have several opportunities to talk with students about the spiritual climate on their campuses. Over and over again I have students tell me that the major negative influence upon the spiritual life at their respective colleges comes from the athletic programs. There seems to be an endless litany of reports of young people being recruited because of their athletic ability, with little regard for their spiritual character. Many of these recruits feel no deep conviction about the so-called Christian commitments of their colleges and view most of the rules and regulations that are normal in evangelical circles as nonbinding on them.

At several of the Christian colleges I visit, the athletes have become a subculture on campus, maintaining a lifestyle that is out of harmony with that of the other students on campus. When the team is predominantly black (as is often the case with the basketball team), and the rest of the student body is predominantly white, this segregation can have all kinds of negative overtones. What I have just described is seldom verbally expressed, but it bears investigation and in my opinion is a growing problem.

All of this might be a bit more palatable if sports were fun for the athletes. But in the majority of cases, even on the high-school level, most of the fun has been taken out of sports. From Little League on up, American sports have become far too regimented to allow for much spontaneous fun. There are the few unusually talented players who never feel threatened when cuts are made and need have no fear of being benched or pulled out of games. But for most, sports hold too much anxiety to be fun. The little boys in their gray-flannel uniforms, wondering if they are good enough to "get in" or scared to death that if they do "get in" they will "mess up," are painful to watch. And it does not stop with Little League. All through their youth, those who play in "organized" sports will spend sleepless nights wondering what will happen to them and whether or not their coaches will give them a fair chance to show their stuff.

As a city kid growing up on the streets of Philadelphia, I was free from most of this painful side of sports. Along with my friends, I played street games that were nothing but fun. It was not that we didn't take our games seriously (although no records were kept and nobody could remember the scores of the games a day or two later), but rather that having a good time was what we were all about.

We had a host of games for which we invented our own rules. These games were played on the asphalt and went by such wonderful names as box ball, wire ball, wall ball, and stick ball. All that was needed in the way of equipment was an old tennis ball. There were no special gloves or uniforms, so rich kids and poor kids could participate as equals. There was never a kid who was left out. Everybody got "picked" and everybody had an equal chance to play. Most of our games could be played with almost any number of players on each team. Sometimes one team would get two average players if the other team got a player who was unusually talented. It made no difference if teams were numerically unbalanced as long as they were fairly matched. I can remember games being stopped and "sides" being rechosen if things seemed unbalanced. The words "no fair" were often heard because if our games were going to be anything, they were going to be fair.

I particularly liked playing touch football on the street in front of my house. There were usually four or five players on each team, and the games would be full of intrigue. Huddles before each play seemed to take forever, because each kid had to be given special instructions which made him or her feel important. Even the player who was not too good at catching the football was given careful instructions. He might be told to "go ten steps, cut left, come back two steps and then go long! I'll fake it to you." No matter that the kid did not catch a pass; his involvement was total. He was so busy counting steps and figuring patterns that he in no way felt left out if somebody else was catching the ball. After all, he was convinced that by being a decoy he had been primarily responsible for the other guy getting free to make the catch. It is no wonder that we never tired of our street games and always felt good about ourselves when play time was over.

It was not until I moved to the suburbs that I discovered how much work play could be. It was in the suburbs that I came across adult coaches who were all too ready to take the fun out of sports for the sake of winning. It was at Little League in the suburbs that I first met coaches who barked at kids like drill sergeants yell at new recruits. It was in the suburbs that I realized sports had to do with how proud your parents would be of you and what your status would be with other kids. It was in the suburbs that sports became a serious business run by adults and devoid of the spontaneity that had been so much a part of my childhood days in the city. I believe that sports must be saved from this kind of perversion. I think that God wants play to be fun—that in the midst of play we might know something of His joy.

I do not want to be accused of "sour grapes" in what I say. Let the record state that I "lettered" in high school and was captain of my college basketball team. But it was no big deal, and that was what allowed it all to be fun. Sports were a joyful diversion for me rather than a preoccupation. Games gave relief from the more serious pursuits of life rather than themselves becoming primary pursuits. I was good at what I did and might have been a lot better if I had not had more important things to do. I had a lot of fun, and that was what seemed to matter most about sports in those days.

I strongly believe that when that which was ordained for joy is perverted into regimented hard work for the sake of gaining status, something godly has been perverted. Christians should protest loudly against such abuses and commit themselves to reclaiming sports to be what God intended for them to be. This may seem like a trivial thing, but I believe that having fun is core to the nature of being saved.

Thus far I have only focused on the abuses of sports that are evident among participants. But something direct must also be said about spectators. I am worried about what watching sports on TV is doing to many families. Are there no limits as to how much time should be spent in watching games on television? New Year's Day could be a wonderful time for family fellowship. Hours could be spent in family visiting. The holiday presents a rare opportunity for meaningful talk with children. Instead, millions of Americans (particularly adult males), disconnect from their families and sit with their eyes glued to television screens to watch a seemingly endless flow of bowl games.

I am sure that there are important dimensions to game watching that I must be missing. But when I consider the hours that are spent watching TV ball games in light of the fact that the typical American father averages only five minutes a day in meaningful conversation with his children, I believe something has gotten seriously screwed up.

It used to be that watching TV sports was something that took up a couple of hours on Saturdays (which was bad enough), but now Sundays have been taken over, and during part of the year Monday evenings are preempted by pro football. (And this is not to mention the all-sports channel on cable.) I am somewhat surprised that preachers do not have more to say about all of this. Ought not the proclaimers of the Word of God to be spelling out what is meant by the biblical admonition, "See then that ye walk circumspectly, not as fools, but as wise, Redeeming the time, because the days are evil" (Eph. 5:15–16).

When I hear sermons on Christian stewardship, the preachers usually focus on what we do with our money. Maybe this is a measure of our materialism. But far more important, as far as I am concerned, is how stewardship is practiced with respect to time. To waste money is bad, but to waste time is worse. You can always get more money, but once time is lost, it is gone forever and can never be recovered. Those precious times that might have been but which were used up in a preoccupation with watching sports events could end up being a source of great regret.

Of all the sins that haunt us, perhaps none will haunt us more than our sins of omission. What you might have done with the time you spent watching games on TV may someday be a most painful recollection. I am not suggesting that watching TV sports is something a Christian can never do, but I am suggesting that you examine your use of time and ask whether or not you have been violating the limits of moderation in this area.

Once again, none of this is meant to be a put-down of sports—at least, not of sports that are truly forms of play. I am convinced that those of us in the evangelical tradition have given too little time and attention to examining the ways in which play can be part of our spirituality. Our theologians have written volumes on the theology of work, but there has been little effort given on their part to developing a theology of play. Certainly *very* little has been written on the theology of sports.

Two books which do give some hint as to the rich insights that await us if we begin to look into the spiritual dimensions of play are Peter Berger's *Rumors of Angels* and C. S. Lewis's *Surprised by Joy.* Of all the things that these two authors tell us about play and sports, what intrigues me most is their insight into how play can provide us with brief touches of eternity and allow us temporarily to experience transcendence. These two authors argue that sometimes, in the midst of play, time and space as we know them become temporarily suspended and we experience life on a higher level or in another dimension.

I know of what they speak. Once I was running the hundred-yard dash as part of the track championships of the city of Philadelphia. The whole event took only a little more than ten seconds for me to execute. Yet those ten seconds were not ordinary seconds; they did not belong to time as I had known it. As I lived them during that race, those ten seconds transcended the normal linear passage of time and took on a special quality that gave me a taste of eternity. Time as it is generally experienced dropped away, and as I ran those hundred yards, the rest of the world did not exist for me. There was no past and there was no future, only the exhilarating, transcendent present. As I recall those ten exhilarating seconds, there seems to be something mystical about them. They did not belong to this life or to this world. The race was run in what theologian Emil Brunner would call "The Eternal Now."

If you cannot grasp what I am trying to say, be sure that there are others who can. Those who in sports have entered another dimension of existence know that there is something of the divine that can be encountered in such moments. If I have not expressed this well, then let me reiterate the words of the ancient Chinese philosopher Lao Tzu, "Those who know cannot say; and those who say cannot know."

Even spectators gain a glimpse of this capacity to experience the suspension of ordinary time and space through sports, although I am convinced they cannot do so in the same manner or to the same degree as the players. The true fan who is watching his or her basketball team in a close championship game with time running out will know what I mean. For your team to have a one-point lead with fifteen seconds left in the final quarter with the other team in possession of the ball is a special existential experience. Time will not be ordinary moments, and the basketball arena will not be an ordinary place. The seconds will belong to another kind of time, and the play will be, in the words of Danish philosopher and theologian Sören Kierkegaard, "suspended in a hundred thousand fathoms of nothingness."

In such a state, time and space in any ordinary sense have been transcended. You are beyond the common world of experience and in a realm where, according to Peter Berger, it becomes easy to believe in the "rumors of angels." This, says Berger, is a taste of transcendence that breaks into our empirical world and lets us gain a hint of reality that is beyond time and space as we know it.

A theology of play is important because heaven is probably more about play than it is about work. We gain a sense that when this life is over we will have ceased from our labors (Heb. 4:11). The afterlife is biblically depicted as a time of celebration and fun (John 7:37). The question is whether or not we who have learned to work with Christ will know how to play with Him. Will we be able to learn how to frolic with the Lord of Creation in play that transcends time and space? It may be that those who cannot play cannot be part of the heavenly kingdom!

There is no question in my mind that playing sports can be a spiritual experience, enabling us to gain a glimpse of heaven. It is only the abuse of this good thing that troubles me. When sports become exploitative and devoid of fun, I am troubled. When the games work against the will of God, I am disturbed. It is when sports lose their goodness that I am saddened. Jesus did not come into the world to destroy sports, but to see to it that the Father's purposes for sports are fulfilled. Christians should preach the will of God on these things because sports are an important part of our lives.

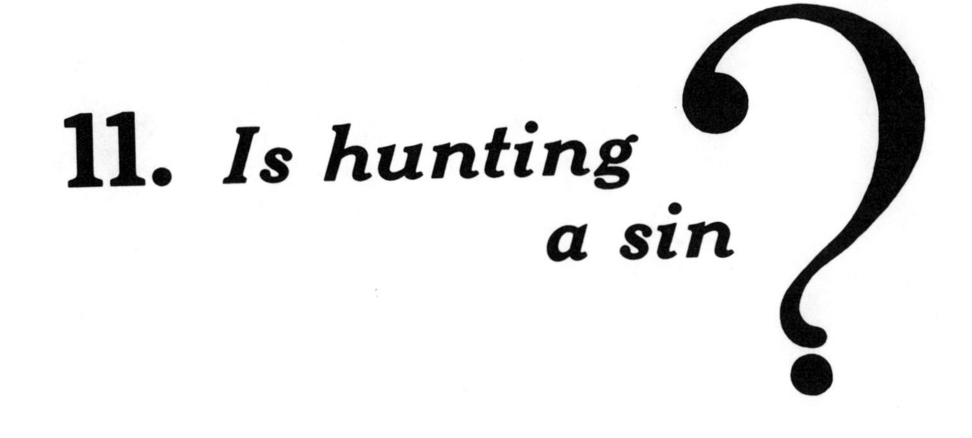
11. Is hunting
a sin
?

MY WIFE AND I stood waiting to board an airplane at the Seattle airport. There in the waiting area by the United Airlines departure gates stood the remains of a huge polar bear. This magnificent creature stood at least eight feet high and seemed to be frozen in time. It had been hunted down and shot by a man whose name was emblazoned on a metal plate—as though there were great honor attached to gunning down such a beautiful creature with a high-powered rifle. My wife and I were saddened by what that man had done. Both of us felt that he had done something very, very wrong by killing such a wondrous creation of God for the sport of it.

I have never been able to figure out those hunters who do not have to hunt for food but simply do it for "fun." I have tried to imagine what emotions that man had experienced when he took away the life of a beautiful animal and made it into a trophy. What did he feel when he pulled the trigger? Did causing the demise of that four-hundred-pound beauty make him feel like more of a man? Did sneaking up on that bear and attacking it with a weapon against which it had no defense really qualify as a sport? Did he derive a sense of pleasure from destroying something alive and beautiful? Was the hunter a Christian and, if he was, did he feel that what he had done was pleasing to God? Did he think that killing that bear was the kind of thing that Jesus would do for fun on His day off?

I am sure many people will agree with me that killing animals for fun is a questionable activity for Christians. But probably most of them will not see the issue as one warranting serious attention. After all, when there is famine in Ethiopia, drug addiction among teenagers in urban ghettos, revolution in Central America, and totalitarian oppression in Albania, the shooting of animals might seem insignificant. However, I am convinced that there is more involved in making hunting into a sport than first meets the eye.

First of all, hunting for the "fun" of it does not take seriously the claim that life is sacred. For some there is a necessity to kill animals for food or in self-defense. But there is a big difference between sacrificing the lives of animals in order to support the lives of humans and killing animals as a form of entertainment.

I am well aware that because we have killed off the natural predators of some animals, we must now kill off a significant number of these animals (such as deer) to keep them from overpopulation and starvation. But I believe that the thinning of certain species in overpopulated areas should be carried out with sadness and not for thrills.

Who can deny that God has created animals, or that His eye is on each and every sparrow that He has made (Matt. 10:29–31)? And who can deny that it is God's spirit that sustains the life of animals and that by His grace they have been put here on this planet? I am convinced that thoughtful reflection will lead most people to realize that all God creates gives Him pleasure and that the destruction of what He loves brings Him pain, especially when that destruction is made into a sport. Why is it that when we destroy something humans have made we call it vandalism, but when we destroy something God has made we call it a sport?

I know that many hunters justify what they do by claiming that getting out in the woods enables them to get away from the highly artificial routines and environments that are so much a part of their urban technological lifestyles. Those of us who spend much of our time rushing between "concrete jungles" in "metallic birds" readily admit that being able to spend time surrounded by the sights and sounds of nature can rejuvenate the spirit and remind us of the joys of a time when life was more simple.

But why is it necessary to hunt to have these experiences? Why must animals be killed in order to enjoy nature? Why not use cameras instead of guns, making photographs that will record that the animals thus captured on film are still alive and free?

I do not need to be told that there are many people who make their living from hunting. Whenever they have the baby seal hunt up in Canada and the Greenpeace people try to stop it, people who hunt for their livelihood are interviewed on the evening news. Inevitably the newscasters are able to find some impoverished Newfoundlanders who claim that clubbing baby seals to death is their only way to make a living.

But even as I listen to the interviews, I ask if there are really no alternatives which would provide them with a viable income. Furthermore, is the fact that an activity provides a livelihood sufficient reason to justify it? I do not accept this kind of argument from urban teenagers who excuse peddling drugs on the grounds that they cannot find jobs or from ghetto girls who sell their bodies because it is the best way to make money!

My feelings on the matter of hunting baby seals are obvious, but I am aware that those who do this are not doing it as a sport. And it is the making of a sport out of hunting that is my primary gripe.

There are those who will say that I just do not understand what people who make a sport out of hunting get out of it. And they are right. There *may* be some need for "male bonding" that is satisfied on a hunting trip. Being together on a hunt may create a wonderful feeling of oneness among the guys. Perhaps hunting gratifies some kind of Nietschean "will to power." I am sure that the psychological motivations for hunting must be complex. But I do not think that I am being overly simplistic when I argue that one of the reasons that Christ came into the world was to make us into new creatures whose basic psychological needs can be met in ways that are nondestructive and harmonious with all the other creatures with which He willed for us to share this earth.

When I was a child, there were two neighborhood boys who outraged our community. They had climbed up a tree, taken some eggs out of a bird's nest, and destroyed those eggs by dashing them against a brick wall. When these boys were asked why they had done it, they horrified all of us with the simple declaration that they were just trying to have some fun. For days people asked over and over again what kind of boys could get pleasure out of such a senseless destruction of eggs. Yet even as a boy, I could not see any difference between boys trying to have fun by smashing those eggs and grown men trying to have fun by shooting birds out of the air! I wondered how my neighbors, many of whom made a sport out of hunting, could condemn children who had made a sport out of destroying eggs.

Once again, I must affirm that I regretfully accept the sad reality that there are situations in which animals may have to be killed. But when the primary motivation for killing animals is sport, I cannot distinguish the moral difference between hunting and the ugly behavior of those bad boys in my neighborhood.

One warm summer day many years ago, I was sitting in a park in Philadelphia. It was during the noon hour, and I was on a lunch break from my job. Sitting on a park bench just a few yards away was a young mother whose preschool children were playing on the sidewalk in front of me. As they played, one of them discovered a group of ants crawling in and out of a crack in the cement. The little girl who made this discovery called to her sister to come and join her. These two children proceeded to gleefully stomp the ants to death. After they had trampled as many of them as possible, the two little girls got down on their knees and began to pick up the remaining insects and squeeze them between their fingers. Their laughter at the killing of those ants had a demonic quality to it. To be frank, I think it *was* demonic; I could sense the Evil One working through them, destroying life.

The cruel demeanor of the girls got to me, and after putting up with their diabolical games much longer than I should have, I yelled "Stop!" The little girls got up and went crying to their mother, who gave me a dirty look for having curtailed what she must have thought was innocent play.

There is little doubt that there are times when we must destroy ants—they destroy gardens and endanger livestock, as well as messing up picnics. Termites must be destroyed lest they eat up our houses. Exterminators must sometimes be called to get rid of cockroaches or mosquitos, who carry disease. Nevertheless, there was something horrible about little girls giggling as they pressed the life out of ants who were not bothering them or anyone else. To them, killing was *fun*—and I find that extremely disturbing.

Every once in a while we pick up the newspaper and read about some old man or woman who has died and left a fortune to be used for the care of a dog or cat. I used to read those stories and shake my head and say to myself, "How ridiculous!" But over the years, my attitudes have changed. I have seen what animals can do for people—especially old people who all too often are bereft of human companionship. Perhaps it is my imagination, but I have seen such empathy develop between some old folks and their pets that it seems to me that the pets and the people begin to look like each other. Just the other day I saw a man walking his bulldog, and everything from the dog's walk to the dog's face resembled the old man who was attached to him with a leather strap.

Studies done by James H. S. Bossard, one of the experts on the socialization of children, reveal that pets can give confidence to children who lack it, security to children who are afraid, and emotional support to many who could not otherwise enjoy life. I have witnessed the special empathy that children can have with animals even as I have seen the camaraderie that can exist between pets and the elderly. I am aware of something sacred going on in such encounters.

I would not hesitate to say that animals are sacramental. I believe that often they can be instruments through which the grace of God is experienced and through which something of God's love for people is enjoyed. Yes, I do believe that people can feel God loving them through animals. It is not *saving* grace (as theologians would say), but it is grace nevertheless. Consequently, when old people leave money for the care of a cat or dog, I understand. I am more aware these days than I used to be of what God can do for us through animals. I am more aware of their sacred function in the scheme of things.

St. Francis of Assisi had no trouble grasping the spiritual significance of animals. The closer St. Francis got to God, the more he found he could commune with animals. The friars who were closest to him noted how often he wanted to spend time with animals; it was said that he actually could talk to them. The most popular artistic portrayals of St. Francis depict him communing with birds.

All of this might seem absurd in our modern scientific world, but it is not. There is ample research to prove that animals know more than most of us suppose they know and often have an uncanny sensitivity to the thoughts and feelings of people. If this were a scientific textbook, I could cite study after study to validate the claim that animals are not so much *less* intelligent than humans as they are creatures with a different kind of intelligence. Animals have been given to us by God not only as food, but in order to share feelings and to generate emotions that we need. We only have an infinitesimal understanding of the role that God has ordained for them to have in our lives. To kill such precious gifts from God as a sport must be sin.

It is interesting to note that animals have a place in the Bible's description of the kingdom of God. Isaiah 11:6 paints a beautiful picture of what it will be like when the *shalom,* or peace, of God is fully known, when even the animals will live in harmony with each other and with all of the human race:

> The wolf also shall dwell with the lamb, and the leopard shall lie down with the kid; and the calf and the young lion and the fatling together; and a little child shall lead them. And the cow and the bear shall feed; their young ones shall lie down together: and the lion shall eat straw like the ox.

I believe, therefore, that those of us who are committed to expressing the lifestyle of God's kingdom in this present time should learn to live in harmony with nature and to love the animals. Those who do not think that animals have a place in God's kingdom should note that when the Bible says "God so loved the world," it is using for the word *world* the Greek word *cosmos*, which embraces not only humans but all the creatures in God's creation. In the eighth chapter of Romans, the vision of God's salvation includes not only those who trust in Jesus, but all that is in God's world:

> For the earnest expectation of the creature waiteth for the manifestation of the sons of God. For the creature was made subject to vanity, not willingly, but by reason of him who hath subjected the same in hope. Because the creature itself also shall be delivered from the bondage of corruption into the glorious liberty of the children of God. For we know that the whole creation groaneth and travaileth in pain together until now (Rom. 8:19–22).

Each year a special church service is held in St. John's Cathedral in New York City. People bring their pets to this service so that they might receive a special blessing. Camels and elephants from the zoo are brought into the sanctuary, and prayers are offered up to God to thank Him for giving us such curious and wonderful creatures. The pastors of the church pray a special blessing on the animals, and the fellowship which God has willed between humans and beasts is affirmed.

Sometimes when I tell people how meaningful this church service can be they laugh. They say that I am being childish. I accept that judgment as a compliment, for I remember that my Lord once said that only those who have become as little children will enter His kingdom. Perhaps part of what He meant was that unless we, like children, believe in the possibility of a special friendship with the animals, we will miss out on many of His blessings.

Woe unto those who kill God's creatures for sport!

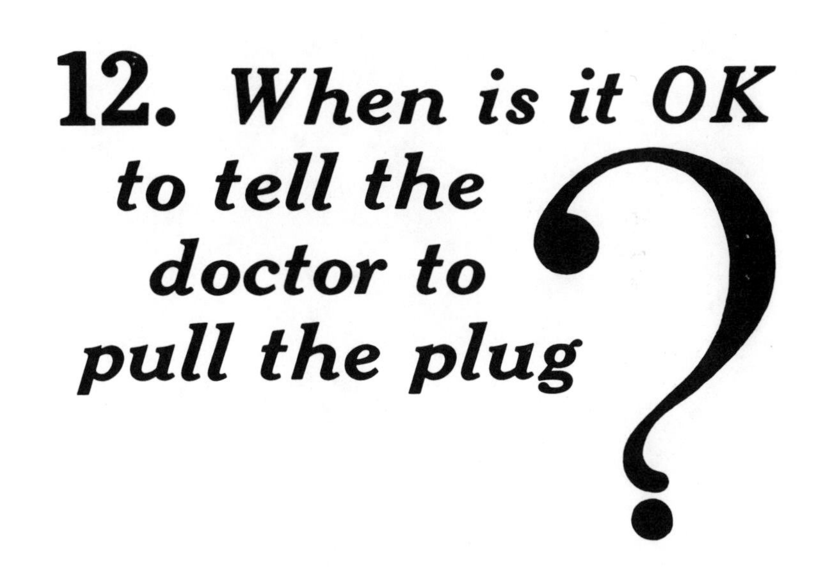

12. *When is it OK to tell the doctor to pull the plug?*

IN THE MOTION PICTURE, *Rollerball,* one of the main characters has an accident in which his head is crushed and his brain is rendered dead. However, the rest of his body organs are still healthy. His heart is still capable of pumping blood. His lungs still have the capacity to process oxygen and expel carbon dioxide. His liver still can process bile and keep his body "clean." All the organs can function with optimum efficiency if only the body is hooked up to machines that provide the electrical energy to keep them going.

This man's best friend, his teammate in the game of Rollerball, has more than enough money to pay the hospital what is necessary to keep the machine going indefinitely—and he decides to do it. He decides to keep the brain-dead body of his friend "alive" in spite of the enormous cost involved. He regularly visits the man who had been his friend, meditating as he sits for hours by the "living" biological remains of a man who once had been the dearest person in the world to him.

Is he doing what a Christian should do? I doubt it—for several reasons.

First of all, there is the obvious matter of stewardship. The money that is being used to keep this insensible body pumping and breathing might be better used. In a hospital in Haiti, children die because there is not enough money to buy basic medicines such as penicillin. In India, young men are immobilized because there is no money to pay for artificial limbs. And in affluent America, there are children with burns or birth defects who will be disfigured for the rest of their lives because they cannot afford the plastic surgery they need. How is it possible to justify huge expenditures to sustain a brain-dead body when the money could do so much for so many of the living?

The economic factors related to sustaining the bodies of persons who have been pronounced brain dead is not just a hypothetical consideration for thousands of families across this country. Recently a friend of mine had to make a life-or-death decision for her husband, who had been rendered brain dead by a disease. Maintaining his body was exhausting the limited financial resources at her disposal, resources that her husband had worked a lifetime to put together. Their hopes and dreams of a college education for her two daughters, as well as her own hopes for a decent life, were wrapped up in those resources. All of a sudden, what had seemed to be a solid basis for meeting the future needs of this family was threatened.

My friend would gladly have made any sacrifice if she had believed there was some hope that her husband might once again be conscious. But such a hope was scientifically impossible. Once the brain dies, whatever knowledge and awareness it held is gone. Brain death is like magnetically erasing the message on a cassette. Once what is there is gone, it is gone forever. When the doctor asked my friend if he should disconnect the machine that was maintaining her husband's bodily functions, she gave her consent. I believe she did the right thing.

Doctors and medical ethicists have thought long and hard about what to do in such instances. Those in the social sciences also have reflected upon the morality of "pulling the plug," as the dilemma is succinctly labeled. I think that what they have to say on this subject can provide help for Christians who have to make hard decisions when loved ones are physically alive but brain dead.

What happens in brain death is that the electronic impulses that run through the brain cells and are essential to the thinking process cease. The cessation of brain waves is registered on an electronic device. No value judgments need be made as to whether or not it happens. When the brain dies, the dial on the electroencephalograph tells us so. And once the brain dies, there is no reviving it. The deterioration of the brain cells starts immediately.

With regard to understanding what makes a person human, social scientists often contend that the conscious interaction the person has with others is of crucial significance. They argue that all those qualities which make humans distinct from other higher primates come through meaningful exchanges with those significant persons who help us to achieve humanness.

When asked to list the traits that establish the infinite qualitative differences between humans and animals, we are likely to come up with traits that are acquired through interpersonal relationships, such as symbolic thinking. We might also include having a conscience to influence our behavior. Some would say that to be human is to have an awareness of self and a consciousness of our inevitable future—which is death. The list could go on and on.

However, when all is said and done, most social scientists would claim that all such traits are taken on by the humanized homo sapien because he or she is caught up in interactive relationships with others. They would claim that individuals become human through a process which they call socialization.

If all this seems a bit too technical, suffice it to say that our humanity is a gift that comes to us from other people. This is not to say that God is not involved. Those who believe that it is God who makes us human simply contend that God does His work of creating our humanity through the agency of the significant other persons who are part of our lives.

If this argument from social scientists is accepted, then we may easily be led to believe that our humanness is so tied up in conscious relationships with others that when those relationships are impossible, as in the case of brain death, what makes us human is gone. All of those qualities which enable us to transcend animals seem to depend upon our having an awareness of others. When this awareness is no longer possible, it may be said that a person is dead.

There are those who argue that none of this takes into consideration whether or not the vegetating body still has a soul. Those who assert this seem to think that the soul is some kind of thing that God puts into people at birth or conception. In reality, biblical scholars teach us that when the Scriptures employ the word "soul," they are referring to the totality of the human personality. A soul is all that an individual becomes in the course of a lifetime, and it is this sum total of a person's humanity, created over the years, which survives the grave. With brain death, the personhood or soul is no longer alive in the body, and it is on this basis that the plug can be pulled and bodily remains allowed to expire.

But brain death is not the only situation in which there is a question of whether or not to turn off life support systems. Even more difficult perhaps, is the situation in which a person who is fully conscious is being kept alive by artificial means and is ready to die.

Beth, the wife of a dear friend, had a disease that rendered several of her vital organs inoperative. She would have died had doctors not hooked her up to an array of machines that kept her alive. Beth was in constant pain. The drugs which were supposed to deaden the pain were no longer effective, and the doctors talked about some kind of surgery that would sever the connections of her nervous system. Beth begged that nothing more be done to her and that she be allowed to die the death that would have been hers were it not for the miracles of medical science. The doctors felt that it was their duty to prolong her life as long as possible, but Beth's husband persuaded them to let her die. He and his wife had worked through the stages of dying and had come to accept Beth's death with grace and faith. The doctors granted her request and, in accord with her husband's agreement with her in this matter, "pulled the plug." I believe that Beth and her husband decided to do the right thing.

In this case, pulling the plug by no means brought about Beth's death. The cause of her death was the disease that had destroyed her body. All that was decided was to stop fighting what God would have allowed to happen had it not been for human interference.

I am not suggesting that interfering with the process of dying is wrong or sinful. That is what modern medicine is all about. Instead, I am suggesting that people do have the right to decide when such interference should end. When continuing life through artificial means causes horrendous pain and exorbitant expense or diminishes the dignity of a dying person, then the decision to keep that person alive seems immoral to me.

Please understand that I am *not* talking about euthanasia, or "mercy killing." Mercy killing requires actively *doing* something—such as giving a pill or injection—to bring life to an end. In Beth's case, the decision was simply to *stop doing* what was prolonging life in an unnatural manner. Mercy killing involves unnatural death. For Beth, death was a very natural thing. Nobody was playing God when the plug was pulled.

Recently a friend of mine received a phone call from someone who was close to her. The caller said he wanted to borrow eight hundred dollars in order to travel to Holland where euthanasia is legal. He had been infected with the AIDS virus and was already experiencing its painful effects. Rather than die a slow and agonizing death, this young man had opted to go to a country where it was legal to receive a painless lethal injection.

My friend, who cares deeply for this young man, turned down his request. She believes that euthanasia is a way of playing God and, therefore, should not be practiced by any of us.

I am convinced she is right. While I understand those who advocate euthanasia, I just do not approve of it. When it comes to human life, I believe the Lord gives it and that only the Lord has the right to take it away.

The church has never accepted suicide or murder, and euthanasia is only suicide or murder by another name. In all of these matters, we must heed Scripture, which says:

> I call heaven and earth to record this day against you, that I have set before you life and death, blessing and cursing: therefore choose life, that both thou and thy seed may live (Deut. 30:19).

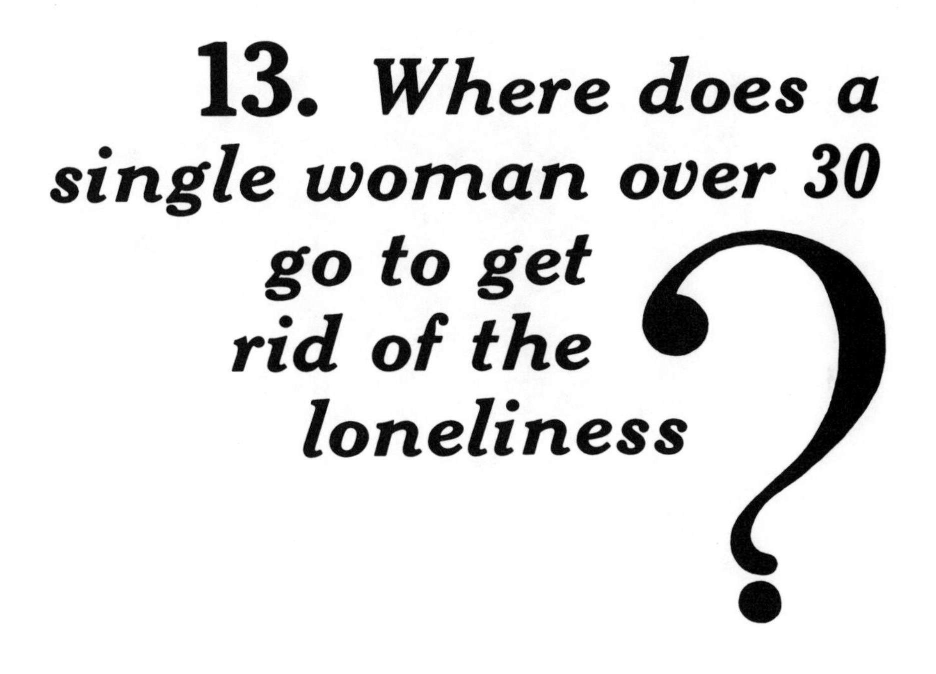

13. *Where does a single woman over 30 go to get rid of the loneliness?*

THE QUESTION THAT FORMS the title of this chapter is not meant to be sexist. I am sure that there are a lot of single men over thirty who are lonely, too. As a matter of fact, studies done on people over the age of thirty reveal that men in this category tend to be more maladjusted and unhappy than are women.

But I raise this question in terms of women because single Christian women in this age bracket seem to have a particularly hard time establishing the kinds of friendships that are essential for a fulfilling social life. The shortage of single men in this age category in the Christian community is even greater than in the general population of the United States. This is partly because women are generally more involved in religious activities than are men, regardless of their age or marital status. Any speaker at any of the singles' weekends or singles' clubs sponsored by churches learns quickly that the available women outnumber the available men by as many as ten to one.

We should not jump to the easy conclusion that the only escape from loneliness is to be found in marriage. While there is much societal pressure to view marriage as the only means for gaining personal intimacy in adulthood, there are other viable alternatives available. It should be noted that we Christians are followers of a single person over thirty who modeled a life of deep and intimate friendship without being married. The church which was established under the power of the Holy Spirit was ordained to provide a level of fellowship for its members that would destroy all semblance of the loneliness that too often pervades the consciousness of Christians. It may not be easy in the midst of the twentieth century to recover the *koinonia* (intimate fellowship) that made first-century Christians into an intimate family of brothers and sisters, but we would be denying the relevance of the Bible for our times if we said that it was impossible.

Every once in a while, social circumstances force people to rediscover the kind of fellowship which might have been normative among first-century Christians. At Eastern College in suburban Philadelphia, I teach in a unique graduate program that prepares

Christians to work among poor people both in Third-World countries and in impoverished communities here in the United States. This program draws students from around the world as well as from all parts of this country. Most of them are single men and women in their late twenties or early thirties.

When the program started, finding suitable housing for these students posed a major problem, which the students themselves helped solve when some of them decided to live in community. Eight of these students found an old four-story house in a rather "worn-out" section of West Philadelphia. With some help from friends, they were able to come up with a down payment for the house. With each of them paying very reasonable rent, they are able to take care of the mortgage payments.

The house is located near a very large apartment building that houses fifty Cambodian refugee families who have made their home in West Philadelphia. Under the leadership of one of the women in this Christian community, an outreach ministry to these Cambodian families has been initiated. The members of the community, all of whom are single, have developed among themselves a deep affection and a strong commitment.

Those members of this group who have completed their degree programs have shown a great inclination to stay in the community and look for ministry opportunities in the Philadelphia area. So far as I can ascertain, those who live in the house are becoming "family" in a spiritual as well as emotional sense. They seem to be gaining a sense of belonging to each other and are escaping the loneliness that so often haunts those who are single in their age bracket.

Living in a community not only allows these single adults to enjoy fellowship with each other; it also enables them to live relatively inexpensively. Eating together as a group makes meals very special times of fun and sharing as well as providing food at a fraction of what they would have to spend if each prepared meals separately. The economy of living in community is particularly important to these Christians because their Bible courses at Eastern College have sensitized them to the need for Christians to live more simply in order to be able to give more to help the poor and oppressed of the world.

As I watch these special single adults develop a lifestyle that enables them both to live out the requisites of the Bible more fully and to escape from personal loneliness, I wonder why churches do not encourage living in Christian community as a good option for single adults.

I realize that the dominant culture promotes an emphasis on individualism which discourages community living, but sociologists and psychologists have long known that such heightened individualism as is practiced in the American socialization process is personally destructive and socially impoverishing. A great many Christian observers of life in America have commented on the need for churches to speak out against this extreme individualism and to offer some paths of escape from it.

It seems to me that promoting Christian community as a way of life for single adults might be a great beginning in this direction. Helping older Christian singles to live in fellowship and love might be one of the most eloquent ways for churches to declare to the world that God calls His people into community. The leaders of the early church would have found nothing strange about Christian singles living together, sharing resources, and delivering one another from the loneliness of individualist living. Actually, I believe they would be shocked that people who have been called into loving community by Jesus would ever live in loneliness.

I realize that there are some who are not prepared to handle the social and psychological strains associated with living in community. But I am convinced that many who think that they would not like it might be pleased to find that they were wrong if they just gave it a try.

I am suggesting that the time has come for churches aggressively to attack the loneliness of singles by being proactive and taking the steps to create community living. Churches should be willing to put up the money for down payments on housing units large enough for a group of singles. They should call singles together and encourage them to see that by living in community they could help each other to grow spiritually and give to one another the emotional support of a Christian "family." Then these communities created by churches could take on particular ministries such as the tutoring of school children with problems or the running of neighborhood Bible studies.

To many, such a suggestion will seem "way out" and dangerous, particularly if the communities established have members of both sexes, as is the case with the one made up of Eastern College students. But I contend that what is *really* "way out" and dangerous is allowing Christian singles to go on their lonely way without doing anything to relieve this suffering.[1]

For singles who are not about to take the bold step of establishing a residential community with Christian brothers and sisters, there are other options for close camaraderie. It is possible to find the kind of fellowship that dispels loneliness by becoming involved in some intensive service project.

For instance, in hundreds of towns and cities across the United States, there are chapters of Habitat for Humanity. This Christian organization is committed to building or rehabilitating housing for poor people who otherwise would have little hope of ever owning their own homes. Unskilled and untrained people join with those who know what they are doing with saws and hammers in order to build and revitalize dwellings for people who otherwise would have to live in shacks and tenements.

Many of the participants in Habitat chapters come from churches, so that Christian singles who get involved will probably find themselves planning and working with people who share their social values and convictions. These brothers and sisters sing and fellowship together. They develop ties that bind. In such a mission, loneliness is often vanquished.

Habitat gatherings provide a much better option for meeting "eligible" singles than do most of those planned "singles' weekends" which are contrived by churches in order to minister to singles. I am not knocking such weekends. I am simply contending that bringing people together for service provides a much more natural setting for singles to interact with members of the opposite sex than do those planned get-togethers which all too easily can become strained.

Habitat for Humanity is only one suggestion, of course. Most communities offer a host of options for Christian service. Try looking for Young Life or Campus Life clubs that need volunteer members. These Christian parachurch groups, which are designed to reach high schoolers, are always in need of older singles who have time and energy to give. Not only is working with high-school

1. A good book on living in Christian community is Dave and Anita Jackson's *Living Together in a World That's Falling Apart* (Creation House, IL: Carol Stream, 1974).

kids exciting, but there is a good likelihood that the volunteer staff will provide peer companionship for the young adults in positions of leadership.

Prison Fellowship, the organization started by Chuck Colson, is also a good opportunity. Those who have trouble relating to teens might find reaching out to adults who have had problems with the law more in their sphere of interest.

My point is that singles who are committed to serving people in need will find themselves in association with others who have a similar commitment. Such meetings have greater potential for bringing together people on the same wavelength as friends or potential marital partners than do most meetings arranged with deliberate matchmaking in mind.

The addresses of the national headquarters for the service organizations I have been discussing are:

Habitat for Humanity
Habitat and Church Streets
Americus, Georgia 31709

Youth for Christ
Box 419
Wheaton, Illinois 60189

Young Life
Box 520
Colorado Springs, Colorado 80907

Prison Fellowship Ministries
P. O. Box 17500
Washington, D.C. 20041-0500

If you write for information about getting involved, in all likelihood you will receive an enthusiastic response listing those persons to contact in the area where you live.

There are those who, while seeing possibilities in the options that I have suggested, still feel that their only real escape from loneliness lies in getting married. Some may argue that this ought not to be—but it is!

Recently, at a weekend retreat for the staff members of an inner-city evangelistic and outreach program, a bright, attractive woman in her late twenties openly confessed her fear that unless she got married she would spend most of her life in painful aloneness.

The staff workers of this organization live together in a large mansion which at one time served as an orphanage. They eat their meals together, have daily devotions together, and go out together socially. Nevertheless, this woman felt a loneliness that her relationships with the other staff members did not take away. She had a loving trust in the other members of the group; if she hadn't, she would not have talked so easily about her needs and her fears. But when she was completely open with herself and with the rest of us, she admitted that for her, marriage was the only real hope for gaining the kind of intimacy that drives away loneliness.

Personally, I am not about to tell such a person that her thinking is all wrong! I believe that I, along with other Christians, should try to meet such a felt need rather than simply tell her something like, "You shouldn't feel that way."

I believe that churches could do more for singles, particularly for women over the age of thirty, in the way of helping them find potential mates. The Jewish community has always established mechanisms to introduce its eligible singles to each other. I doubt that there is much likelihood of a viable Christian matchmaking service in the near future. (The few attempts at this that I know of have proven highly inadequate.) But church people could spend more time and effort in "fixing up" their single friends. Since few decisions in life can affect the spiritual condition of a person more than the choice of a marital partner, helping a friend locate a suitable Christian date might well have eternal consequences.

Such a practice would present a far healthier option than the "bar hopping" route, although more Christian women allow themselves to be reduced to this than we care to imagine. One day when I was in New York City, I stepped into a bar on Second Avenue. (I was late for an appointment and there did not seem to be an available phone anywhere else close by.) As I sat in the phone booth making my call, I noticed an attractive woman enter the bar, take her place on the stool, and send out the signals that she was available. It did not take long for some guy to "move" on her and complete the conditions for a pickup.

I had to walk by the two of them as I left the bar. They were too busily engaged in "making time" to notice me, and for that I am glad, because I recognized her. Just a couple of months earlier she had been in my office seeking counsel, hoping that I would be able to suggest some ways for her to meet somebody to date. Alternate ways of escaping loneliness had not seemed to be live options to her; after listening to all of my suggestions, she had still seen getting a man as her only hope. Obviously, I had not been very helpful, and in her loneliness, she had sought other ways to solve her problem. Becoming a pickup in a bar is degrading for any woman, but it must have been particularly distasteful for this woman, because she was a Christian.

It is far too easy to condemn such "cheap" behavior without any understanding of the frustration and loneliness that is often part of the plight of the over-thirty single women who seem to abound throughout Christendom. I wondered if this particular woman might have been spared this degrading "bar hopping" if I had taken the time and effort to engineer some dates for her. I wondered whether I could have made a major difference in her life if I had enlisted some of her friends in such an effort.

There is one additional suggestion that I am reluctant to make because for many it comes across as extremely devious and to others it appears somewhat degrading. Nevertheless, allow me to say that a good place for a Christian woman to find a mate is in Bible college or seminary. While the ratio of men to women in seminaries may be changing, the single men in seminaries still significantly outnumber the single women. Consequently, if a woman who is committed to Christian service sees marriage as the most desirable way to overcome her loneliness, then it is a good idea to go to a place which will optimize her possibilities.

In seminary there is an opportunity to get to know people on a deeper level than just dating or meeting casually. The discussions in seminars, the talk sessions at lunch, and the sharing in class projects all provide good opportunities to get beneath the surface of a classmate's personality and to discover partners who share ideas and values.

Sociologist William M. Kephart has long made it clear to those of us in family studies that institutions of higher education play a crucial role in mate selection. Such a significant number of those attending college end up married to fellow students that parents would do well to consider this factor when helping to choose the schools their children will attend. Parents are wise to help their children choose colleges where they are likely to meet a suitable mate, because there is a 30 percent probability that their children will marry partners they meet in their collegiate setting. While I do not have exact percentages, I believe that the same is true for those who are older. Seminaries in particular often bring together people who have the same cultural and religious backgrounds and who are also likely to be on the same intelligence level.

I am well aware that this suggestion will create some negative reactions. But of all the people between twenty-five and thirty-five years of age whom I have counseled because of loneliness, those who have followed this advice have had the most positive results. I find nothing wrong with persons who put a premium on being married making a conscious effort to be in places where they have the best chances to meet persons who are of the same heart and mind.

Sometimes, of course, things do not work out like we wish they would. Many a person who has prayed to be married has had to come to accept his or her singleness. While the individual who very much wants to get married is likely to consider the failure to find an acceptable partner a serious disappointment in life, it is not a disappointment which is lacking in positive potential.

Singleness, according to the apostle Paul, is an ideal state for those who want to maximize their ability to serve Christ. Single persons are usually more in a position to give long hours in service to others than are married persons whose mates and children require vast commitments of time. That is why he wrote:

> But I would not have you without carefulness. He that is unmarried careth for the things that belong to the Lord, how he may please the Lord: But he that is married careth for the things that are of the world, how he may please his wife. There is a difference also between a wife and a virgin. The unmarried woman careth for the things of the Lord, that she may be holy both in body and in spirit: but she that is married careth for the things of the world, how she may please her husband. And this I speak for your own profit; not that I may cast a snare upon you, but for that which is comely, and that ye may attend upon the Lord without distraction (1 Cor. 7:32–35).

On the mission field I have found that Roman Catholic nuns and priests are much more able to go to difficult places to live and serve than are Protestant missionaries who have family obligations.

My own missionary society, the Evangelical Association for the Promotion of Education (EAPE), is 90 percent staffed by single people. I regularly praise God that He has given these workers the grace to live in singleness. In their singleness they can take more of the risks that go with working in inner-city ghettos, and they can afford to give the time that is often essential to help boys and girls who have little parental involvement in their lives.

I have tried to write this chapter out of my own experience in knowing and counseling single persons over thirty. Obviously, my answers are not comprehensive. I did not discuss the possibility of a single person's finding another Christian with whom to share an apartment and establish a binding covenant of friendship. I did not explore the ways in which single persons can have wholesome friendships with married couples. I did not develop the ways in which churches can make efforts to integrate singles into their larger circles of fellowship.

What I *did* try to do was to explore some new options. My suggestions may be controversial, but I did not make them in order to start arguments. I made them because I have seen them work. If you are single and lonely, they may work for you.

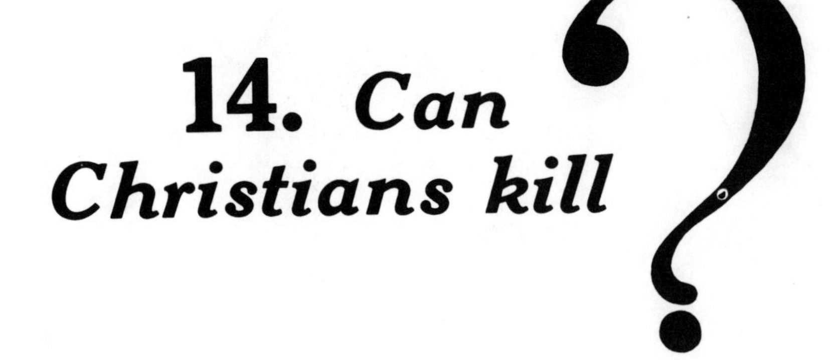
14. Can
Christians kill

WHEN I WAS IN HIGH SCHOOL, my mother gave me Charles Sheldon's novel, *In His Steps*. Its message was simple but powerful: *To be a Christian is to do whatever Jesus would do if Jesus were in your situation facing your options*. And to me that message was crystal clear. I was to study the Bible and learn of Christ. I was to pray and get so in tune with Christ that I would increasingly think as He thinks and more and more know what He would do. I took that message to heart and became committed to being an imitator of Jesus.

During the Korean War, the draft was in effect, and there was some indication that I might be required to go into military service. In a preliminary session at the draft board office, I was interviewed by an army colonel. He was obviously concerned about me after I gave several indications that I might have problems about killing in battle. I distinctly remember that colonel looking across his desk at me and sternly asking me why I had doubts about the rightness of killing for my country. I told him about reading *In His Steps* and said I was trying to figure out what Jesus would do if He were in my shoes. The colonel asked me directly, "Do you think you could shoot at another human being or drop bombs from an airplane?"

I answered, "If I got into a plane and flew over an enemy village, just before I pulled the lever to release the bombs, I would have to ask, 'Jesus, if you were in my place, would you drop these bombs?'"

The colonel answered me gruffly, "That's the dumbest thing I ever heard. Everybody knows that Jesus would never drop bombs!"

Perhaps that colonel knew more about the nature of Christ than most theologians and preachers I have known. There was no doubt in his mind that the incarnate Christ would never drop bombs. I think he was right. And I believe it follows that if Jesus would not drop bombs, then those who claim to be His followers are obligated not to do so either.

When I was in seminary, there was much discussion in our theology courses about the nature of Christ. Our intellectual exchanges explored such strange and erudite concepts as His ontological nature and His existential ground of being. But with all of our theological discussion, we never answered this basic question: Would Jesus drop bombs?

It is no wonder that so many people in their thirties and forties have come to think that religion is irrelevant to what really matters in life. They were the ones who had to go off and kill in Vietnam without their churches' ever having provided them with an answer as to whether or not Jesus would kill if He were in their places. It is no wonder that so many of them came home psychologically shattered. These veterans had had to pull triggers and drop bombs without ever having resolved the question as to whether or not they were being good followers of Jesus.

There are those who would cite passages in the Old Testament wherein God ordered the people of Israel to liquidate their enemies and even to practice genocide. The protagonists for war can bring up story after story to prove that in ancient days, God not only approved of war but ordained the slaying of Israel's enemies. To be perfectly frank, I must admit that those Old Testament passages have always troubled me. My high view of Scripture prevents me from simply dismissing them, as some of my colleagues have done, as representations of a consciousness that had not yet grasped the highest insights which might be achieved in the evolution of religion.

But one thing is clear to me, and that is the fact that Jesus declared that the days of retributive justice were over. In the Sermon on the Mount, he carefully informs us that we are not to return in kind any evil that our enemies might carry out against us:

> Ye have heard that it hath been said, An eye for an eye, and a tooth for a tooth: But I say unto you, That ye resist not evil: but whosoever shall smite thee on thy right cheek, turn to him the other also. And if any man will sue thee at the law, and take away thy coat, let him have thy cloak also. And whosoever shall compel thee to go a mile, go with him twain. Give to him that asketh thee, and from him that would borrow of thee turn not thou away. Ye have heard that it hath been said, Thou shalt love thy neighbour, and hate thine enemy. But I say unto you, Love your enemies, bless them that curse you, do good to them that hate you, and pray for them which despitefully use you, and persecute you (Matt. 5:38–44).

Whatever might have been the law before, Jesus declared specifically that He was giving us a *new* commandment. And I take Him at His word. When He said *new,* I believe He meant *new.* That means that what He was commanding was different from the old commandment that had governed the ways in which the Jews reacted to those who committed crimes against them. I am convinced that in the Sermon on the Mount, Jesus was deliberately introducing a new set of ethical standards that far transcended anything that had been taught by Moses.

The laws of Moses outlined in the Torah (the first five books of the Bible) were without doubt the embodiment of the highest concepts of justice the world had known prior to the coming of Christ. They were laws that made the punishments for evil deeds equal to the crimes. This was a departure from much of what went on in the ancient world where punishments and retribution usually went far beyond what would have been parity or justice. In retaliation for injury or hurt, people in Bible times often retaliated without restraint. Punishment, instead of fitting the crime, was often so extreme that the punishment itself became criminal. It was over and against this tendency toward excessive punishment that the Mosaic Law was given. The word of the Torah was that punishment for wrongdoings should be just recompense. This justice was an expression of the will of a loving God.

With Jesus, however, a new law was given. Jesus carried us beyond the Mosaic law as He called us to love our enemies and to do good to those who hurt us, "That ye may be the children of your Father which is in heaven: for he maketh his sun to rise on the evil and on the good, and sendeth rain on the just and on the unjust (Matt. 5:45).

The love of God which was evident in the Torah had its ultimate expression in the teachings of Christ. In this sense the new law of Christ did not abolish or do away with the love of God so evident in the Old Testament, but fulfilled it in its final form. Christianity is a new and better way of life, and it is a way of life that I believe rejects violence and the taking of life as a means of creating the kingdom of God. As much as I understand what Christ is about, this makes killing, whether by capital punishment or in war, exceedingly questionable for those of us who claim to be followers of His way of doing things.

When I went to see the movie *Ghandi,* I came away with an eerie feeling. It was the strange awareness that this Hindu leader understood and applied the teachings of Jesus more faithfully than do most Christians. His nonviolent responses to the oppression which the people of India had to endure at the hands of their colonial overlords was a direct consequence of his reading of the fifth, sixth, and seventh chapters of the Gospel of Matthew. His decision to love his enemies was a decision to live out what he had learned from the teachings of Jesus.

There are those who argue that the nonviolent style of Ghandi worked only because he was employing it against the humane English. They say that if this strategy had been used against Nazi Germany it would have failed, because nonviolence against brutal enemies will, in the end, prove futile.

In response to this argument I must point out that nonviolent resistance *did* work against the Nazis. As a matter of fact, it was the only strategy that had even limited success in stopping Hitler's demonic persecution of the Jews. In Denmark, when the order was given for all Jews to display their ethnic identity by wearing armbands displaying the Star of David, something remarkable happened. The king of Denmark himself put on one of the armbands and walked among his people. When the citizens of Copenhagen saw their king identify with the Jews, they followed his example. Soon Danes everywhere were wearing the Star of David. The people of Denmark let the Nazis know that they were at one with the Jews, and that whatever evil the Nazis wished to perpetrate against the Jews they would have to also perpetrate against the Danes. This brave action defied the armies of Hitler, and when the chips were down Hitler had to back off.

I wish things were always as simple as what happened in Denmark during World War II. The reality is that history is strewn with the bodies of those who have loved their enemies. Nevertheless, a direct application of the teachings of Jesus has led many to willingly lay down their lives in love rather than to return evil for evil. Those who follow this heroic commitment are deserving of praise, and praise is just what Jesus gives them when He says,

> Blessed are ye, when men shall revile you, and persecute you, and shall say all manner of evil against you falsely, for my sake.

> Rejoice, and be exceeding glad: for great is your reward in heaven: for so persecuted they the prophets which were before you (Matt. 5:11–12).

Assuming a nonviolent posture in a violent world may get us crucified, but it is only those who are willing to be crucified in following Jesus who can fully call themselves His people.

One final concern that moves me away from taking human lives, either in war or as punishment for extreme criminal acts, has to do with the way I read Matthew 25:40:

> And the King shall answer and say unto them, Verily I say unto you, Inasmuch as ye have done it unto one of the least of these my brethren, ye have done it unto me.

I take this passage quite literally. I am well aware of the fact that many credible biblical scholars differ with my interpretation of these verses, but I am convinced, nevertheless, that whenever I look into the eyes of another human being, it is possible for me to encounter Jesus looking back at me. I believe that Jesus stands on the other side of every person whom I meet face to face and that He chooses to present Himself to me through those persons. In the context of every human relationship, if I choose to do so, not only can I encounter Jesus, but I can hear him saying, "What you do to this person, you do to me." And I believe that if we come to think like this, we will find it impossible either to kill in battle or to accept capital punishment. If we believe that what is done to "the least of the brethren" is done to Jesus Himself, it becomes impossible to deliberately kill anyone.

Those who differ with the way I interpret Matthew 25 usually contend that when Jesus made this statement He was referring only to those who were Christians. I find that hard to believe since the basis for becoming a Christian (that is, accepting salvation through the death of Christ and the infilling of the Holy Spirit) had not yet been established when these verses were written. But even if this limitation were to be accepted, there is good reason for Christians to refrain from killing despite the fact that sometimes societal ethics seem to justify it. Even if we limit the meaning of these verses to apply only to Christians, there is still a case to be made. I think that the following story makes this case better than anything I could add here:

> There was once a young monk who lived in a monastery in southern France. Of all his hopes and dreams, none was more important than his desire to see Rome—the Holy City. He constantly implored the abbott of his monastery, and one day the abbott gave in and gave him permission to make the trip.
>
> Arriving in Rome was something of a culture shock for the young monk. The awesomeness of the city, the sophistication of the people, and the obvious secularization of the church left him confused and upset. One day, as he was wandering aimlessly through the streets of the city, he became aware that large numbers of people were making their way to the Coliseum. Not understanding the language, he could not inquire about what was going on. He simply joined the flow of the crowd, and shortly found himself seated in the arena, waiting for the "show" to begin.
>
> Onto the floor of the Coliseum marched several dozen soldiers. Taking their places, they turned in militaristic style towards the place where Caesar was seated. They lifted their swords, saluted the emperor, and spoke the traditional words, "We who are about to die salute thee!" The soldiers then paired off, facing each other, poised for the signal that would initiate their duels to the death.
>
> It was then that the young monk realized what was happening. He stood and yelled at the top of his lungs, "In the name of God, stop! In the name of God, stop! In the name of God, stop!" But the roar of the crowd drowned out his voice.
>
> He ran down the aisle to the barrier at the edge of the Coliseum floor, and screamed at the gladiators again, "In the name of God, stop! In the name of God, stop! In the name of God, stop!" But, if they heard him, they ignored him.
>
> It was then that the young monk leapt over the barrier onto the floor of the arena and poised himself between two of the gladiators. To each of them in turn, he yelled, "In the name of God, stop! In the name of God, stop!"
>
> The gladiators, angered by the young man, instinctively ran their swords through him, and his dead body fell to the ground in a crumpled heap. The gladiators, shocked by their own brutality, stood motionless. The crowd in the Coliseum rose to its feet in stark silence. Then, in a dramatic stillness, one man left his place high in the stands, made his way down the aisle, and left the Coliseum. Another did the same, and still another followed. The stream of people leaving the Coliseum turned into a river, and soon the amphitheater

was emptied. Caesar himself slipped away; the gladiators put up their swords and solemnly left the field of battle.

Never again would there be gladiator fights in the Coliseum at Rome. The killing had come to an end—all because a young Christian monk had the courage to stand up in the midst of murderous insanity and yell, "In the name of God, stop!"

We have heard the Christian debate on the pros and cons of militarism. Most of us have endured with patience the sophisticated arguments of theologians on this matter. But when all has been said, I am still left with the sense that what is really needed in this age of brutal killing is for all of us to join that young monk and to scream at the top of our lungs, "In the name of God, stop!"

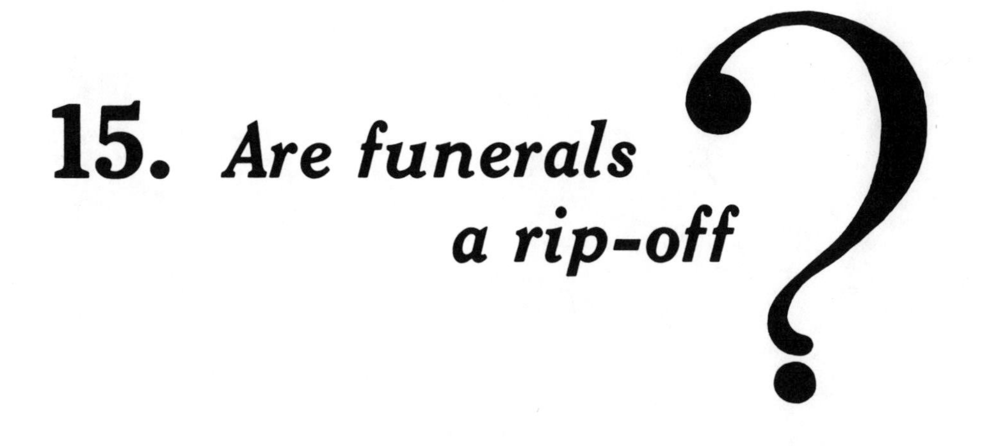

15. *Are funerals a rip-off?*

FUNERALS CAN BE memorable events that honor the memory of the dead. But they can also be rip-offs that leave the living friends and relatives of the deceased feeling hurt and exploited.

In the extreme, there is the story of a West Virginia mining disaster that occurred some years ago. Scores of poor men lost their lives. The mining company approved a small legacy for each of the surviving families, hoping that the gifts would provide some alleviation of what would be certain poverty. However, before the bodies of the dead miners were cold, unscrupulous undertakers swooped down on the community. These merchants of death played on the frayed emotions of the surviving family members and sold them on expensive funerals which took almost everything they had.

Of course this is a negative caricature of the modern-day undertaker, and we must be careful not to paint the profession with a broad brush. In most instances, those who are retained to oversee funeral arrangements are relatively sensitive people who want to help the grieving family go through a difficult time with a minimum of emotional discomfort. And yet, regardless of those intentions, many of their clients later conclude that the undertakers they trusted got them to spend more for the funeral than they should have.

When I was a pastor, I regularly went with widows and widowers to funeral homes in order to make arrangements for burials. And I often felt constrained under such circumstances to mutter suggestions to the bereaved to resist what I felt were cheap manipulations by undertakers to get them to buy things that seemed to me to be unnecessary and even ludicrous.

For instance, I worked hard to dissuade an economically pressed widow not to buy a foam rubber mattress for her dead husband, in spite of the undertaker's claim that the mattress would be providing a comfortable rest for the corpse for all eternity. I also balked when this same undertaker tried to sell the widow an expensive airtight vault for her husband's casket which was "guaranteed to keep him dry." My pleadings notwithstanding, the widow spent a bundle on such things and was left with only a pittance from her husband's insurance money.

Once again, I do not want to suggest that such practices are the norm. But these sorts of things happen often enough to make people like me a bit wary.

My questioning of contemporary funeral practices also involves the fact that undertakers are more and more living up to the new name they have adopted for themselves—"funeral directors." Now, I am not simply trying to save a prerogative for a clergy that already has lost a long list of them. But it is my contention that the direction of Christian funerals should be solely in the hands of the church leaders—clergy or lay. (This would not even be an issue for Roman Catholic priests, who have always maintained control over what takes place at a funeral.)

I firmly believe that funeral services should be religious ceremonies that enable all concerned to reaffirm some age-old truths about death and resurrection. They should be times in which carefully structured rituals give to all concerned a sense that the familial and friendship ties generated by the dead will be maintained and revitalized. Funerals should be times of rededication to high and holy beliefs and values. As such, funerals should be directed by those who are appointed to lead us in such thoughts and commitments.

With all due respect to undertakers, on the whole they are not usually experts in such things. Nevertheless, too often undertakers take it upon themselves to establish the entire scenario for funerals and, in many instances, only call the clergypersons involved after all the arrangements have been made.

In one instance I know of, the announced time of the funeral was in conflict with a wedding the pastor was scheduled to perform. The undertaker let it be known that this was the only time available to him and if it were impossible for the pastor to make it at that time, he would have to find someone else. By that time it was too late for the bereaved family to change undertakers, and they had to go through this difficult time without the comfort that the pastor might have provided. This would not have happened had the pastor been in on things from the beginning.

Often, too, even the ways in which the clergy are to participate are dictated by the undertakers. Ministers at times are told where and when to speak and how long they will have for their "remarks."

At the end of the funeral, the undertaker's slipping an envelope containing the honorarium to the minister provides a further indication as to who is running things and who is a hired participant.

In all fairness, I must add that undertakers probably need to perform this "funeral director" role for unchurched families. But I firmly believe Christian funerals should be different. They should be planned carefully and as far in advance as possible, rather than leaving it to be done at the time of death, when there is a high level of stress. There should be discussions with other family members and careful consultation with the clergy who will be asked to conduct the funeral. Consideration should be given to what truths ought to be conveyed, what Scripture should be read, and what hymns should be sung.

Certainly the costs of the funeral should be discussed, and the discussion should focus upon how the cost of the funeral will reflect upon the Christian commitment to stewardship. Careful thought should be given to the good that could be done with money that is all too easily squandered in loving gestures to the dead who are no longer able to appreciate them. Would it not be better to honor the dead by giving money that would have been spent on an expensive funeral as a gift to Mother Teresa for ministry to the old and sick, or to feed hungry children through some worthy organization such as World Vision or Compassion International? Furthermore, do not expensive funerals and burial vaults suggest something about the finality of death that we Christians do not believe to be true?

Among the things that ought to be decided ahead of time is whether or not it is right to bury good body organs which could benefit people who desperately need them.

As medical science improves the techniques of transplants, more and more transplant patients are living full and productive lives. Unfortunately, a shortage of donated organs is causing a situation in which more and more people are denied transplants because donors are unavailable. I know of a young mother who died long before she had to, leaving three small children, simply because she needed another heart and there was none available. Thousands upon thousands of people could be delivered from pain and early death if only kidneys were willed for their use. One of my former students, the pastor of a small church in upstate New York, died for lack of a kidney transplant. Stories of this kind are innumerable. Is it right for Christians who face death to ignore these needs? Are transplants not in accord with the will of God? Ought not churches to urge their members to sign up with those hospitals and medical organizations which arrange for transplants?

Eye hospitals have a desperate need for corneas. Why should good eyes be buried with the dead when they can be instruments of sight for the living? Ought not eyes to be willed to the eye banks of hospitals to be made available to those who need them?

What is left of the body after transplantable organs are removed can also be a blessing to others. Organs and bones which are not used as transplants can be donated for teaching purposes and for research. Skin can be used to aid in healing severe burns. Medical students are in great need of the bodies of the dead in order to prepare to serve the living. Cadavers are at a premium in medical schools, and it seems to me that churches should urge Christians to meet that need.

My wife and I have signed the necessary papers to have our bodies used for the good of others after we are finished with them. We carry cards in our wallets so that if either of us should die suddenly away from home, those who are left with our remains will know what to do and whom to contact.

We are convinced that this is what God would have us do. However, we had to figure this out with no help from the preachers we have heard or the books we have read. What to do with the bodies of the dead is not the sort of question that is usually dealt with in theological seminaries. It is not the kind of concern that gets written up in books that are bestsellers among religious people. It is the kind of unpleasant, but very important, issue that most people want to avoid and therefore seldom consider until it is too late.

The big question people raise with me when I tell them what my wife and I have decided to do with our bodies upon death is, "What will there be to resurrect from the grave when Jesus returns?" And it is true that the Bible *does* speak of the resurrection of the body. The idea that a disembodied soul floats around heaven throughout all eternity is not a biblical idea. If anything, the Bible teaches that those who live after death do so in some corporal fashion.

When Jesus was resurrected from the grave, He could say to doubting Thomas,

> Reach hither thy finger, and behold my hands; and reach hither thy hand, and thrust it into my side: and be not faithless, but believing (John 20:27).

That Jesus was bodily resurrected from the grave was attested to by the empty tomb and is the cornerstone of orthodox theology.

The apostle Paul goes on to tell us,

> But if the Spirit of him that raised up Jesus from the dead dwell in you, he that raised up Christ from the dead shall also quicken your mortal bodies by his Spirit that dwelleth in you (Rom. 8:11).

Paul explains that the bodily resurrection of Jesus not only guarantees that death can be conquered, but also lets us know that those who are "in Christ" will themselves have a similar kind of resurrection. We are told that beyond this life we shall live again and have bodies that can be seen and handled.

Paul lets us know that our new bodies will not be subject to sickness and decay:

> So also is the resurrection of the dead. It is sown in corruption; it is raised in incorruption: It is sown in dishonour; it is raised in glory: it is sown in weakness; it is raised in power: It is sown a natural body; it is raised a spiritual body. There is a natural body, and there is a spiritual body (1 Cor. 15:42–44).

But Paul also tells us that our new bodies will be glorious transformations of the bodies we presently possess—and for many that is the rub. There are those who ask how our bodies can be resurrected and transformed after the manner of our Lord if parts of them are implanted in others, chopped up by medical students, and otherwise scattered across the face of the earth.

I must honestly say that I have not the slightest idea. But I am convinced that the God who once created us out of dust will be able to recreate us out of the dust that we may one day become, no matter how far and wide that dust may have been scattered. After all, He is God. Consider the fact that the overwhelming proportion of those who have died throughout human history have become scattered dust regardless of how they were buried! The Bible says as much: "All go unto one place; all are of the dust, and all turn to dust again" (Eccles. 3:20).

I once asked my wife what I should do with any parts of her body that remained after medical science had used whatever it found suitable. I asked her if I should have those limited remains buried or cremated. She humorously responded, "Surprise me!" I do not mind joking about the remains of her body or of mine because the sadness of death is swallowed up in glorious resurrection according to the Word of God:

> And as we have borne the image of the earthly, we shall also bear the image of the heavenly. Now this I say, brethren, that flesh and blood cannot inherit the kingdom of God; neither doth corruption inherit incorruption. Behold, I shew you a mystery; We shall not all sleep, but we shall all be changed. In a moment, in the twinkling of an eye, at the last trump; for the trumpet shall sound, and the dead shall be raised incorruptible, and we shall be changed. For this corruptible must put on incorruption, and this mortal must put on immortality. So when this corruptible shall have put on incorruption, and this mortal shall have put on immortality, then shall be brought to pass the saying that is written, Death is swallowed up in victory (1 Cor. 15:49–54).

It is obvious from what I have written that undertakers would have a hard time making a living if my advice were to be taken seriously by most Christians. While I wish the many good people who are in this business no ill, I would like funerals to be expressions of good Christian stewardship. So far as I am concerned, it would be a good thing if the money spent on expensive caskets and funeral arrangements were to be spent to alleviate the sufferings of the living and the money usually spent on flowers be designated to the mission work of God's kingdom.

At the same time, I do not want to suggest that the passing from this life be handled without ceremony. I believe that there *must* be a memorial service—that rites of passage are essential to mark the important transitions of our lives. And I believe that it is of crucial significance that the loss of a loved one be commemorated in a way that honors that person, enables the survivors to handle grief, and ritualistically unites those persons who were held in relationship with each other by the love of the one who has died. Without a ceremony to do these things, death would be made even more difficult to handle and much of what the deceased person had lived for might be lost or overlooked.

Before my mother died, she worked out the details of what was to occur at her funeral. She selected the hymns she wanted sung and the scriptures she wanted read. She gave me clear instructions about what she wanted me to say about her and provided her pastor with careful directions as to what to say about her resurrected life.

My mother was one of those persons who constantly engineered the gathering together of all the members of our extended family. She wanted her memorial service to be a time in which all of us would be present to honor her by committing ourselves to be in touch with each other on holidays and other special occasions. Her plans and hopes were realized at that service, and we have followed through on what she had hoped we would do. That memorial service marked a renewal of the commitment of those of us who remained behind to love each other and to keep in touch. So far as I am concerned, that memorial service was far superior to the typical funeral when it came to allaying sorrow, and it was much more Christian.

If you are interested in donating your organs at death to others who need them, here are some places you can contact:

Humanity Gifts Registry
130 S. 9th Street
Suite 1550
Philadelphia, Pennsylvania 19107
(215)922–4440

Lions Eye Bank of the Delaware Valley
9th and Walnut Streets
Philadelphia, Pennsylvania 19107

Delaware Valley Transplant Program
2401 Walnut Street
Suite 404
Philadelphia, Pennsylvania 19103
(215)543–6391
(To contact this organization from any part of the country, call 1–800–Kidney 1)

United Network for Organ Sharing (UNOS)
P.O. Box 28010
Richmond, Virginia 23228
(800)446–2726

North American Transplant Coordinators Organization (NATCO)
5000 Van Nuys Boulevard, Suite 400
Sherman Oaks, California 91403
(818)995–7338

American Council on Transplantation
4701 Willard Avenue, Suite 222
Chevy Chase, MD 20815
(301)652–0994

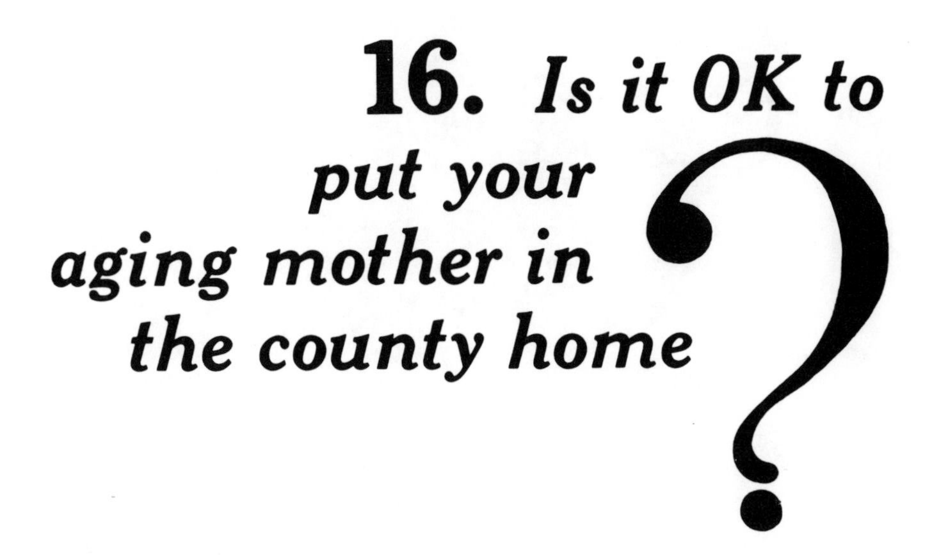
16. Is it OK to
put your
aging mother in
the county home
?

ON THIS ONE, allow me to argue both sides of the question. First of all, let me give you some of the reasons why the answer might be "no."

Twenty-five years ago I accepted the pastorate of a church with about four hundred members in suburban Philadelphia. Shortly after taking up the duties of this position, I was handed a list of "shut-ins" who needed visits from me. At the top of that list was the name of an elderly woman who was in the county-sponsored home. I made it my first duty to go there and visit her to let her know that her church was concerned and praying for her.

When I arrived at the home, I went to the reception desk and asked where this woman could be found. The receptionist went through a stack of index cards and came up with one for the woman about whom I had inquired. On that card was the record of all those who had visited her during the previous few years. I was surprised when the receptionist told me that mine would be the first visit that this woman had had in six months. The reason I was surprised was that she had several relatives who lived within a few miles of the county home, and some of those relatives were faithful members of my church. I found it hard to believe that these church people would fail to visit their elderly relative who resided so close to them.

The receptionist explained that such is often the case because, as she sadly pointed out, friends and relatives find that visiting is painful for them and sometimes creates more guilt than they are able to handle. I was not quite sure I understood this explanation, but I inquired no further. The receptionist told me how to get to the ward where my church member had her bed, and I hurried on my way.

I got to the ward and immediately was overcome with an extreme discomfort about what I saw. The ward was clean enough; as a matter of fact, it was sterile. The walls were covered with white tile, and the linoleum floor was spotless. Along each wall was a row of beds. Later I counted them and discovered that on each side of the room were twenty beds with twenty elderly women waiting to die.

The nurse on duty pointed out a bed about three-quarters of the way down the ward where lay the woman I had come to visit. I walked briskly in her direction, trying not to see the other women. I did not want to see them. There, in broad view, was one frail elderly woman sitting on a commode. I was shocked. I hoped she had not noticed that I had seen her. She had, no doubt, lived most of her life in an era of Victorian values, and I thought she would be horrified to realize she had been viewed in this condition by a young man.

However, there was no need for my concern. The old lady was not in touch with reality. She was babbling incoherently and seemed to be totally indifferent as to where she was and what she was doing. I would later wonder how much of her senility and psychological detachment was the result of old age, and how much of it was her only defense mechanism against conditions that must have offended every sensitivity that she ever had.

When I got to the bedside of the woman I had come to visit, she seemed to be in a trance. Her eyes were open, but they stared blankly and saw nothing. Her mouth hung open, and she lay there motionless. She was clean. Everything about her was clean even her completely disheveled hair was clean. But she just didn't seem to be "there."

When I spoke to this woman, however, the blank stare vanished. She blinked her eyes and slowly turned her head toward me. I told her who I was and why I had come, and she smiled. And then, much to my surprise, she spoke to me in a clear and intelligent manner. The two of us talked for about half an hour. During that time, I learned that she was not bedridden, but simply lay in bed for the better part of each day because she could think of nothing else to do.

When I came to the end of my visit, I asked her if she would like me to pray for her. She nodded an affirmative answer, and when I asked what she would like me to ask of the Lord, she replied, "Ask Him to take me home!" This sad lonely woman wanted to die, and I could not blame her.

The second time I visited the county home to see the same woman, I happened to arrive at noontime. While I was seated by my friend's bed, I noticed that the nurse had come into the ward pushing a cart on which were stacked the meals for the day's lunch. The nurse took one of the lunch trays from the cart, carried it over to the first bed in one of the long rows of beds, set it down on the small table, and began to feed the occupant. I was disturbed by what I saw and heard. I watched the nurse prop the old woman up in the bed, pry open her mouth, and start pushing food into her. After forcing each spoonful of food in, the nurse would yell out, "Swallow!" The poor old woman rather mechanically tried to obey but obviously had no real interest in eating. Much of the creamed corn that was being shoved into her reemerged from her half-closed mouth after each spoonful. The food ran down her chin and onto her clothes, but neither she nor the nurse seemed to notice.

I watched this process in silence, but when I saw the same treatment being handed out to the woman in the next bed, it was too much for me. I got up and went over to the nurse and asked, "Is what you are doing really necessary? Couldn't you make eating a bit more pleasant for these women?"

The nurse stopped what she was doing, stood up, and confronted me face to face. Her answer to my question was an abrupt, "Yes!" She went on to say that this was not her idea of a good time. She explained that she had thirty women to feed and an hour and a half to do it. A number of the women were unable or unwilling to feed themselves. All of this meant that what I had considered such ugly treatment of the elderly was that nurse's only choice. This county home, like most, was understaffed, and this meant that the elderly women on the ward either got fed in the dehumanizing manner I had just observed or were not fed at all.

The nurse, realizing that I was a minister, went on to say, "If you want to change things around here, why don't you bring some of the women of your church down here once a week so that they can help me to feed these people right? It won't solve the problem, but it will give a few of my friends here a chance to have a decent meal." The next Sunday I asked the leaders of the women's missionary society at my church to do just that. They thought it was a good idea, but they never got around to doing it. I guess it is always easier to raise money or make up gift packages for people on the other side of the world than it is to spend time with the desperate people who are close at hand.

What I have described is not meant to disparage the county home. It was clean, and most of the people who worked there really did seem to care for the elderly who were in their charge. The food was better than might have been expected at a place like that. All the basic necessities of life were given. And yet, the whole scene seemed horrible to me. I came away hoping that I would not have to go to a place like that to waste away and wait to die. I hoped that I would not have to endure being left there by those who cared for me but had lives of their own to live. My experience at the county home left me with the strange hope that, should I reach a time when I could no longer care for myself, I would either drop dead from a heart attack or be killed instantly in some kind of accident.

The second scenario that I want to give you describes a family that decided to care for their elderly father at home rather than have him put away in an institution. These were good people who swore that they would never "let poor old dad spend his last years in one of those places."

For the first few years the old widower did quite well and actually added some social spice to the life of the family. He had a keen wit, and his stories from "the good old days," whether truth or fiction, provided some entertainment for his two grandsons. But then something very sad began to happen. The old man began to show the signs of Alzheimer's disease. Little by little he lost touch with reality. The time came when he seldom recognized his own son and daughter-in-law, and eventually he did not even know who he was.

Other things went wrong. The constant presence of repulsive odors throughout the house gave ample evidence that the old man had lost control of his bowels. Eventually he had to be diapered, and his daughter-in-law was often left with the unpleasant task of cleaning him up after his "accidents." The home became a dismal place. The boys, who by this time were in their teens, stayed away as much as possible and never brought their friends to visit. The caring couple that had undertaken this venture of love began to experience tensions; the joy that had been so much a part of their marriage seemed to be gone. Being unable to leave their father alone denied them the occasional nights out that are so essential for keeping a marriage fresh and lively.

Money was now a real problem for the old man's loving children, and arguments over money became increasingly frequent between them. The health-insurance benefits often available to those who are in hospitals could not be collected because this poor man was being cared for at his son's home. Expenses for the help needed to care for him proved more than this heroic family could bear. While it was seldom discussed, the couple was aware that the money that might have been available some day to educate their two boys was being slowly used up.

The whole situation became sadder than I can put into words. I could not help but ask myself if it would not have been better to have put the man into the county home. Does not the Bible tell us that no other human relationships should take priority over the maintenance of the well-being of a marriage? Does not the apostle Paul admonish those who get married to cleave to each other even if it means forsaking all others—even one's parents?:

> For this cause shall a man leave his father and mother, and cleave to his wife; And they twain shall be one flesh: so then they are no more twain, but one flesh (Mark 10:7–8).

There is a third scenario I would like us to consider before we attempt to come to a conclusion as to how to handle this increasingly common problem. It is the way of the Hutterite community. The Hutterites are a group of Christians who are very much a part of the Anabaptist tradition, which some church historians have aptly called the "Radical Reformation."

The Hutterites, like their Mennonite brothers and sisters, are committed to living out the values and dictates of the Sermon on the Mount (Matt. 5–7). They accept the concern for the poor that requires financial sacrifice and the love for enemies that leads to pacifism. Unlike their Mennonite friends, however, they have decided to live in Christian communes. This practice was derived from their attempts to work out in their own lives the lifestyle of Christians described in the second chapter of Acts. One such commune called "The Bruderhof," located just north of New York City, has become home for a significant number of these Hutterites as well as for a number of Christians from other denominations who identify with the Hutterite lifestyle.

The Bruderhof is economically self-sufficient. Its people grow their own food and provide income for the community by working in some fairly profitable cottage industries. There are communal meals, regular community socials, and worship gatherings. And there is a common acknowledgment that all are responsible to care for all. There is a commitment among the members to be a family.

In The Bruderhof, the care of the elderly does not fall to the nuclear family. Instead, the entire Christian community assumes this responsibility. The community serves as a kind of extended family in which the elderly are seen as the mothers and fathers of everyone. The advantages of such an arrangement are more than obvious. No single married couple is financially taxed should an elderly person become bedridden and in need of costly medical care. No single couple is physically exhausted from the care required by the elderly father or mother. There are not the overwhelming time demands that are experienced by an individual or couple endeavoring to care for an elderly parent outside such a communal setup.

Actually, care for the elderly enhances the meaning of the word *community* among the members of The Bruderhof. The empathy and concern which all the members show increases each person's dignity and self-respect. In short, the care of the elderly, even when they are sick or feeble, becomes a joy and a privilege. The Bruderhof allows the children to "honor" their mothers and fathers as the Bible requires without having to undertake on their own a task so demanding that it may well have debilitating effects on their other relationships.

There are many who would argue that the Hutterite solution to the problem is quaint but unrealistic for most Christians. They would claim that the concept of The Bruderhof does not fit in with the way of life prescribed by modern American culture.

Of course there is much validity to this point of view, but before we dismiss the Hutterite plan too quickly, perhaps we should ask ourselves some important questions. Is the lifestyle prescribed for Americans such that, by accepting its norms, we are forced to abandon certain Christian responsibilities—such as home care for elderly parents? If this is the case, is not opting to live an alternative lifestyle such as that of the Hutterites reasonable?

Has raising Christian children in the context of a culture molded by the values and thinking patterns forced upon us by television become impossible? If so, is it not reasonable to raise our children in some kind of environment that goes against the flow of the dominant culture?

Has the heightened individualistic lifestyle, with its emphasis on accumulated personal wealth, created a world wherein a refined version of the "law of the jungle" prevails? Then why does it seem unrealistic to choose to live in a Christian community in which people contribute to one another insofar as they are able and receive from one another as they have needs?

In a society which offers a cultural religion that seems to contradict everything Jesus set forth in the Beatitudes (Matt. 5:3–12), is it not reasonable for Christians to want to live in fellowship with those who desire to live out the Sermon on the Mount?

I think that it is fair to say that most of us reject the lifestyle of community lived out in The Bruderhof *not* because it is an unreasonable Christian response to the ways of the world, but because we are too much in love with the world and refuse to leave its earthly pleasures. But as we turn our backs on the way of life expressed by The Bruderhof, let us be honest enough to admit that we may be rejecting one of the few societal systems that provides dignity and well-being for those elderly family members we claim to love.

Obviously, the question as to whether or not to put an elderly parent in the county home has not been forthrightly answered. And we have not even mentioned all the other options for care that are available to older people who can afford them. However, it should be obvious that no answer can be given in a categorical fashion. My personal bias would tend in the direction of keeping the elderly out of nursing homes, but I acknowledge that my bias toward caring for the elderly at home may be more the result of my ethnic Italian upbringing than biblical imperatives.

Regardless of what we do for the elderly, there are certain things that should be borne in mind:

(1) *Elderly men and women should be in an environment in which each has a say in what happens to him or to her.* Too often keenly aware elderly people are denied the opportunity to make those decisions that determine their own destinies. They should have the right to determine who their doctors and nurses should be. They should be allowed to decide what kinds of food they want and to regulate the quality and amount of their food. They should be free to make their own hours and to go and come as they please. All of this, of course, is conditional upon their being able to do such things. But when such privileges are usurped

unnecessarily, senility and physical disintegration will also increase unnecessarily.

(2) *The elderly must not be shut off from the mainstream of life in society.* They should be in situations where they have the opportunity to interact with people of different ages and in different settings. To be confined to only a small homogeneous group for all social gratification can be emotionally depressing.

(3) *The elderly are entitled to be treated like adults.* That may seem like a strange request, but sociologists have long noted that older people are often talked to as though they were little children. Go and visit a nursing home sometime. Watch and listen to how the elderly are addressed. The vocabulary, sentence structure, and subject matter of the talk these old people must endure are too often like those which are used in conversations with four-year-old kids. Furthermore, sociologists have long been aware that the way in which a person is treated greatly influences what that person becomes. We must wonder how many of the elderly act like little children because they have been defined as little children by those who care for them.

(4) *Last, we must always remember the words of the apostle James, who told us that we do not have true religion unless we have a religion that motivates us to regularly visit the widows and widowers of the world and express to them our love:*

> Pure religion and undefiled before God and the Father is this, To visit the fatherless and widows in their affliction, and to keep himself unspotted from the world (James 1:27).

What that means is quite clear. The elderly must never be neglected by the Christian community. We must always be looking for new ways in which to make them feel a part of our lives.

One successful experiment in creating humane care for senior citizens is taking place in Florida. Twice a week, children from a day-care center are bused over to spend the day at a home for the elderly. The children very much enjoy the individualized attention that the elderly give them, and the old folks, on the other hand, get a real kick out of playing games and listening to the endless chatter of the children. Some special relationships have grown up between these two different generations, and members of both have been blessed.

In another creative effort I know about, some elderly widows who otherwise would live quite isolated lives in their respective homes are picked up each morning by a van and brought together in a church recreation hall. These women come out of a German Mennonite background in which sewing and needlework skills were very much encouraged. At the church, they join together to use these skills, which otherwise might be neglected, to make magnificent quilts. Their work is incredibly detailed and artistically brilliant.

Once a year, these quilts are sold at public auction for very good prices. Buyers come from hundreds of miles around to take part in the sale. The money raised from the selling of the quilts is then given to the missionary work of their denomination. Thus, the creativity of the older women is preserved and respected, mission work is increased, and—perhaps most important—these women have endless hours of enjoyable visiting time as they work together.

Another good idea is for a church to establish day-care centers for the elderly. Increasingly, there are churches which provide places for grown children to drop off their elderly parents in the morning and then pick them up in the late afternoon. This enables these elderly folks to continue to live with their children, who may be employed during the day, without being too much of an imposition. Sometimes churches also make "sitting" services available for the elderly so that those who care for them are able to have evenings out for entertainment. Such programs make it possible for people to keep their elderly parents at home and still live normal lives.

Arrangements like these can work out very well except when the elderly are very sick or so weak that they must be confined to bed. It is then that some kind of nursing home facility may be the only answer. But even when that happens, the elderly should be cared for in the name of Christ. By making sure that they are visited by different people of the church each week and by maintaining a flow of greeting cards and phone calls, we can insure that the elderly can continue to feel a real part of the Christian community. Bedridden or shut-in old folks can be called upon to be "prayer warriors" for other members of the church and in that way continue to be a vital part of the church's life.

I once visited a North Dakota town where a congregation paid special attention to an elderly woman who for years had been a stalwart of her church. When she was put in a nursing home, they visited her and phoned her with great regularity, and they assigned her the task of praying daily for every member of the church.

I was informed that it was the custom to have special speakers who preached at the church stop by the nursing home and visit her, so I did. When I stepped into her bedroom, she looked up at me from her pillow and asked in her delightful Norwegian accent, "*V*y have you come? Have you come to talk about Jesus or the *v*ind, the *v*eather, and the *v*iskers on my chin?"

This bedridden woman was busy at work carrying out her prayer responsibilities, and she was willing to take time out from her important task only as long as the time would be spent in talking about her Lord. Even though she was confined to a bed, the people in her church had found a way to keep her actively involved in their lives.

It is generally acknowledged in our country that we have an "aging population." Longer life expectancy and a decreased birth rate mean that in years to come a greater percentage of the population will be elderly. This means that the problems of caring for the elderly are going to become greater and greater as the years go by. We must find better ways of handling this problem, because right now the options for care do not look too attractive for most of us.

Maybe the place to begin is to start today doing for the elderly what we would like done for us when our time of old-age confinement comes up. With regard to caring for the elderly, "The Golden Rule" is our best hope, and it would be wise for us to set about living out this principle right now.

Think about it. Pray about it. Do something to make a difference in the life of at least one elderly person today.

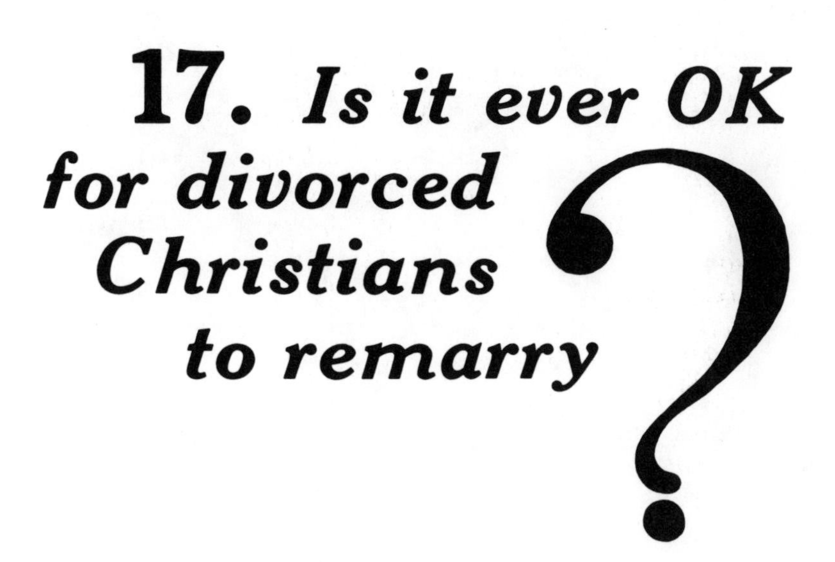

17. *Is it ever OK for divorced Christians to remarry?*

IF YOU ARE OVER FIFTY years of age, you can remember when divorce was a rarity among Christians. Furthermore, when church members did get divorced, they seldom remarried. They were convinced that to remarry while one's former mate was still alive was to enter into an adulterous relationship:

> And he saith unto them, Whosoever shall put away his wife, and marry another, committeth adultery against her. And if a woman shall put away her husband, and be married to another, she committeth adultery (Mark 10:11–12).

Twenty-five years ago, no bonafide fundamentalist pastor would perform marriages if divorced persons were involved. People in a marriage where one of them had a living former spouse were thought to be "living in sin" and had a hard time gaining membership in most evangelical churches. Certainly, divorced persons could not possibly be pastors of churches. Broken marriages disqualified ministers forever from holding forth the Word of God from the pulpit.

Times *have* changed! Today divorce has become common among evangelicals, and some of the most prominent fundamentalist leaders and television evangelists are on second (and even third) marriages. Over the last few years it has become a rarity for a church to refuse membership to a couple because one or both of them have been divorced.

Personally, I believe that we have become all too casual about accepting divorce and hence have created a social milieu in which people with troubled marriages use divorce as an easy out. In earlier times, those in difficult marriages felt restrained to stay in them by society in general and by the church in particular. Usually those who were socially pressured to stay in marriages which seemed far less than ideal made the best of their situations and put a great deal of effort into making them better. Often they succeeded in making something good happen and were able to look back on their decision to stay married as a good one. Most sociologists believe that the pressure once exerted upon married couples to remain married was a help to those who needed encouragement to stick it out through hard times. Societal pressure encouraged married couples to stay together and work to create positive love relationships rather than to seek an easy escape from interpersonal tensions.

I personally believe that most married couples inevitably come to a time when they wonder why they ever got married in the first place and think that it would be a relief to be "free" again. There comes that morning when the guy wakes up and looks across the bed to see his wife still asleep, her hair hanging down over her face and her mouth half open, and he asks, "How did I get into this?" Or perhaps she wakes up first to see her unshaven husband with (as in my case) *no* hair hanging down over his face, and she asks, "Is this what I'm stuck with for the rest of my life?"

I believe it may be what one decides at that first moment of disillusionment that determines whether or not the marriage will succeed or fail, be happy or sad. If two people *decide* to make their marriage work in the face of disappointment and confusion, they probably will succeed. I believe that it is the task of society and certainly the responsibility of the church to keep people married by creating a climate in which the decision to make the marriage work is the expected one.

Another belief of mine, with which some of my colleagues in the social sciences concur, is that divorce is contagious. It appears to me that when a couple gets a divorce, it is not long before their close friends are following suit. Consequently, I am sad to say that I often find it necessary to warn married people to be very careful about their relationships with those who have had divorces and who view their divorces in positive ways.

That may seem unchristian, as newly divorced people are often in desperate need of Christian friends who will lift their deflated egos and provide them with positive means of escaping from loneliness. However, if those who are divorced speak glowingly about their recovered freedom and consider their divorces to be among the smartest things they have ever done, beware. They will have a negative influence upon those who are having difficulties in their own marriages. If divorces are seen as happy solutions to the troubles in marriages, they become attractive options for others to adopt.

Furthermore, there may be an unconscious tendency for divorced people to encourage friends who are going through marital tensions to also get divorces so that those who are already divorced may escape from a subjective sense of being deviant. What is crucial is the attitude of those who are divorced. I can see no problem if they view their divorces as tragedies and if they look on those who are able to save their marriages as fortunate. It is only when divorced people are cynical about marriage and positive about divorce that they become dangerous for married people to be around.

I do not want to give the impression that all marriages should be maintained—no matter what. Obviously there are some marriages that ought to be ended because they are destructive and/or dangerous. Most of us are aware of persons for whom marriage is a life-threatening situation, when one partner is being physically abused by the other. It would be foolish to suggest that these women stay with their husbands unless those men are willing to get the kind of professional help that will enable them to overcome such brutalizing tendencies. Even then, exacting care must be exercised, because psychological counseling does not insure a high rate of success among those with this problem. Those who would argue in absolute terms that the biblical admonition is for wives to be submissive to their husbands in spite of such circumstances are using Scripture as a club rather than as a guide. Those many women who have been conned into staying in marriages where they were subjected to regular beatings because they had been led to believe that such loyalty was required of Christian wives have been badly served. I believe that in such situations divorce, while extremely regrettable, is just, and it would be wise counsel to encourage abused spouses to get out of these kinds of marriages. And there are times when the same counsel must be given to victims of psychological abuse.

There are others who ought to get divorces because ending their marriages is essential for the psychological and physical well-being of their children. Many children have had to endure sexual abuse and other forms of dehumanizing treatment because parents have maintained marriages that ought to have been ended. I know of one particular case in which a mother who knew that her husband was sexually abusing her preadolescent daughter did nothing more than beg him to stop. She stayed married to the man in spite of her daughter's ongoing pain simply because she had been taught it was her duty as a Christian wife to remain with her husband until death did them part.

It must be noted in such cases that the Bible speaks specifically not so much against divorce as it does against remarriage—which I will speak to later in this chapter. I believe that the Lord affirms the right to divorce when there is overpowering evil that will continue as a result of one's staying in the marriage.

Sometimes Christian people are divorced against their wills. Given the state of contemporary divorce laws, Christians can find that their mates are able to get out of marriages and into new ones without their consent or cooperation. Needless to say, there can be no condemnation of those who are pushed out of marriages through no decisions or desires of their own.

There is some evidence that the apostle Paul went through such rejection. We know that Paul was once married, because the Bible tells us that he was once a member of the Sanhedrin, the ruling body of Jewish society, and membership in the Sanhedrin was contingent upon being married. Paul, who was definitely unmarried by the time he wrote the epistles to the church at Corinth, may have been widowed. But there are many scholars who suppose that when he went through his radical conversion from zealous Pharisee to committed Christian, he alienated his one-time wife. It has been suggested that she left this man who, because of his spiritual transformation, had become a complete stranger to her.

I have a friend, a brilliant college professor, who has had an experience that parallels what might have happened to Paul. She and her husband were secular humanists who shared an agnostic attitude toward God. Then one night at three in the morning, she woke up and was overwhelmed with the powerful awareness of the presence of God. My friend, who is now a Pentecostal, found herself "praying in tongues" and praising this God who just a few hours earlier had been completely unknown to her. When in the morning she told her husband about her awesome spiritual encounter, he was not the least bit impressed. As a matter of fact, he was convinced she had "flipped out" and needed psychiatric treatment. Not being able to understand or even sympathize with her newfound faith in Christ, he grew increasingly distant and antagonistic toward her. He became interested in another woman who was on his own academic and antireligious wavelength, and he divorced his wife to marry his new "friend." The divorce was hardly the doing of this Christian woman who still hopes that her husband will come to know Christ.

I believe that divorced persons still have responsibilities and obligations to their former spouses. This is in contrast to the beliefs and practices of ancient days. In Bible times, divorce was the prerogative only of husbands, and once they declared themselves to be divorced, they had no obligations to their former mates. Wives could be abandoned with no means of support. Disgraced by their rejection, it was not uncommon for their own families to refuse to accept them back. Often such women were reduced to begging and sometimes to lives of prostitution in order to survive. I am convinced that part of the reason that Jesus was so strongly opposed to divorce was that He had witnessed the sad condition of such victims of divorce and was furious at the lack of concern for their welfare.

This indifference to former mates is evident in less dramatic forms in today's world. I am amazed when I see how little concern there often is among divorced people for their former mates. All across America there are men who have abandoned their former wives and their children to lives of economic privation and struggle with nary a thought about how they are doing. Increasingly, abandoning families in such a manner is practiced by women, too. It is beyond my understanding how persons who were once intimate can become so disconnected that they have no regard for each other's well-being.

I believe that when we are married, we are married *until death do us part.* To me that means that when people take the wedding vows, they make a commitment to care for each other for the rest of their lives. Thus, even if these people cannot live with each other (which seemed to have been the case for such a notable Christian as John Wesley, the founder of Methodism), the obligation to provide for the care and well-being of one's mate remains a firm requirement. Even after a marriage is legally ended, Christians are not divorced from looking after their former spouses. Thus, care for former marital partners is viewed as a responsibility to be carried out regardless of what the other person does. For Christians, a marital breakup does not mean a divorce from loving concern and service. I know this is not a widely held view, but it seems to me that such obligations are wrapped up with the marital vows and that even divorce does not end them.

And that, of course brings up the tantalizing question as to whether or not Christians who have suffered a divorce can ever remarry. Some have argued that in one place in Scripture there seems to be some approval for divorce, providing the case is adultery.

> And I say unto you, Whosoever shall put away his wife, except it be for fornication, and shall marry another, committeth adultery: and whoso marrieth her which is put away doth commit adultery (Matt. 19:9).

When such is the case, they contend that remarriage is a viable option.

This attitude scares me because often adultery is a reaction to neglect, and the person who appears wronged may be more guilty than we are apt to see. Many people are driven to divorce by unloving mates who deflate their egos and make them easy prey to adultery with any who will build their self-esteem.

Furthermore, I am worried over the possibility that such teachings will make people too ready to seek divorces in the face of unfaithfulness. Vast numbers of marriages that have been hurt by adultery have been healed. I also worry that some may see implied in this particular doctrine that adultery means the end to a marriage when it does not have to be.

I have struggled with the question of the remarriage of divorced persons perhaps more than any other of these difficult issues. When I was serving as a pastor, the issue was raised unpleasantly time and time again.

On the one hand, I knew the teachings of Christ and had a desire to be uncompromising in holding to His words on this subject. On the other hand, I always came back to the painful reality that what I believed put a major proportion of the population both inside and outside the membership of the church beyond the realm of God's grace.

There were just too many lonely Christians who needed partners. There were no Christian communes to carry them through life in a context of loving fellowship (maybe there ought to be). There was little hope for ongoing care for them in later life. All that some of these divorced people could envision for their futures was an old age of aloneness in some cheap apartment. The church should and could offer singles something better, but it does not. And I found it difficult, if not impossible, to pronounce sentences of loneliness on such socially hungry people.

When divorced Christians fell in love and came to me to perform their wedding ceremonies, I was always perplexed. In so many cases, the pat answer that I had learned from my fundamentalist teachers in Bible college did not seem right. Sometimes, after much inner struggling and still filled with doubt, I would decide to perform the ceremonies.

Looking back on such decisions I realize now that I took too much authority upon myself. I should have taken these matters to the deacons of my church and asked them to make those decisions *with* me. I *do* believe that there are circumstances that warrant remarriage, but I think that deciding when it is good and right to go ahead and perform the wedding ceremonies may be too arbitrary a decision for one person to make, and that it would be better decided by the authority of church leadership. Each case should be analyzed, studied, and prayed about by the leaders of the church along with the pastor. I believe the decisions about remarriage should be made on a case-by-case basis. The failures and sins that led to the ending of the earlier marriages should be examined, and repentance, when in order, should be made. The couples to be married should be well aware of the heavy deliberations and struggles that go on. There must be no hint of a "taken-for-granted" attitude.

The reason that I suggest this plan is that I want to hold two important beliefs in diametrical tension. On the one hand, I want to communicate that our God is a God of second chances and of forgiveness. On the other hand, I want people to understand that the principle of lasting marriage is to be upheld.

What I have suggested may give the church the opportunity to do both of these things. Allowing remarriage for divorced persons only after prayerful deliberation and approval by the leaders of the church gives hope for remarriage without taking the whole process too lightly. This is a way of affirming people who need another chance while not accepting without question the belief that divorce and remarriage is a right of Christians.

When all is said and done, I tend to be more accepting of remarried divorced persons than a strict adherence to biblical codes might allow. There may be those who will use such a statement to attack me as some kind of theological liberal who has abandoned the teachings of Scripture. But before such judgments are made, perhaps the following real-life case should be considered.

A couple came to me explaining that they were in a horrible predicament. Each of them had been married before and then divorced. They had met at a ski resort in Colorado, fallen in love, and married. They had brought three children into the world and had a well-established family. A year earlier, both of these people had become Christians and were now seeking to live in obedience to Scripture. They had come across the teachings of Jesus on this subject and were very much under conviction.

They wanted to know what they should do now. Should they separate, since living together could be said to be living in adultery? And what could they do about their former mates, since in both cases these persons had remarried and had children in their new marriages.

I prayed with this couple and urged them to seriously repent of the mistakes and sins which had led to the ending of their former marriages. They did so. There was even an effort on the part of each of them to contact their former mates and plead for forgiveness. For the husband, the approach made to his former wife was most constructive. She was married and along with her new husband had become a Christian. The confessing of the sins which had led to the divorce provided great release for all concerned.

I went on to tell this troubled couple that the grace of God was sufficient to cover what had happened. This did not make the new marriage "right" in the fullest sense, but I told them that God would cover whatever was wrong. I told them that this was what the grace of God is all about. And I believe that!

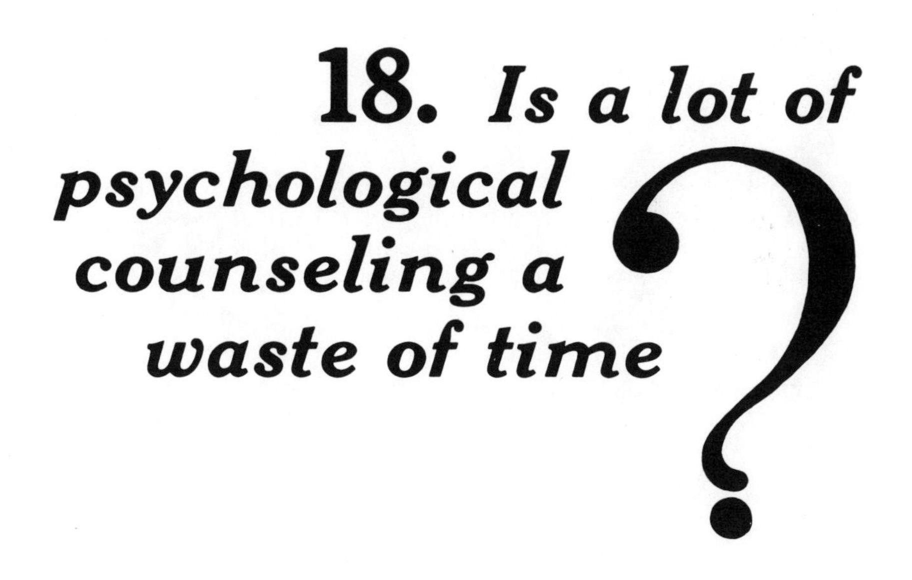

18. *Is a lot of psychological counseling a waste of time?*

IT SEEMS AS THOUGH people are more mixed up today than ever. We modern Americans are in worse shape psychologically than any other people on the face of the earth, and we seem to be getting worse with every passing day. Suicide rates are up, depression is our most common ailment, marital breakups are accepted as normal. More and more people are turning to drugs and alcohol to escape their painful lives, and psychiatric institutions have waiting lists.

Messed-up emotions and mixed-up minds are not evident only *outside* the church. The psychologically confused are not simply worldly folks who just need a good dose of the gospel to straighten them out. Church people are themselves caught in the morass and mire of psychological problems. The people of God need help, too. Some of our most prominent evangelists have condemned psychotherapy and psychiatric treatment as unnecessary for Christians and then found it necessary to seek "professional help" themselves because of serious personal problems.

So common are psychological problems among religious people that most ministers find that functioning as amateur psychologists is part of their role as counselors. Clergypersons who find the problems people bring them too difficult to handle often refer those people to psychotherapists and psychoanalysts. There is an assumption that these "scientifically trained professionals" will be able to pull off the miracles that the ministers, who lack such training, consider to be beyond them. There is the unspoken belief that those with academic degrees in one or the other of these specialized fields of psychological healing know what they are doing and can be expected to solve most problems. Unfortunately, we are learning the hard way that a good number of those in the psychological helping professions are at best ineffective and at worst harmful. We are coming to learn the hard way that sometimes the counseling people receive from the professionals makes them worse instead of better.

By no means do I want to put down all professional counseling—quite to the contrary. I want to urge people who have need for counseling to get it. I want those for whom depression has become unbearable to know there is help out there. I want those who are having marriage problems to be assured that there are good counselors available who can guide them to happier lives. I want those who have self-destructive tendencies to be informed that there are people who can show them how to overcome what troubles them.

Several years ago, some dear friends of mine had come to the verge of getting a divorce. The whole situation was particularly upsetting to my wife and me because they were very close to us and we had always viewed them as a solid Christian couple. They went for professional counseling, but that accomplished very little.

In retrospect I see that the reason that counseling was so ineffective was that the counselor they chose was ineffective. His personal style of counseling and his theories of human personality, which dictated the therapy he employed, combined to make the counseling experience for this couple totally ineffective.

However, by God's grace my friends found their way to a second counselor, who had a very different approach and a very different style of therapy. Today, this couple is making significant progress toward putting their marriage back together again. Both of them are discovering negative things about themselves that had been bottled up for years. As these things are being brought out and dealt with, their counselor is certainly being used by God to do something wonderful for my friends. This is just one case that demonstrates how good professional counseling can get.

I want to make clear in this chapter that help *is* available, but that if you are to get the help you need, you must be very careful about where you go to get that help. You must be sure that the professionals to whom you turn have a sympathy for the Christian faith, hold a biblical view of human nature and the sources of human problems, and do not make psychology into a religion. A lot of the psychological help that is being offered by degree-holding, approved professionals is phony. A lot of it is anti-Christian and quite capable of destroying people.

It is important that we distinguish between the various forms of help available to people when they are in psychological trouble. First of all, there is *psychiatry*. This discipline may offer the best hope for helping those who are having serious problems. Psychiatrists are medical doctors and thus, when necessary, can make medication part of the treatment for their patients. Often the psychological sicknesses of people are caused by things that are wrong with them physically. Psychological depression, for instance, can sometimes be traced to a chemical imbalance in the body and can be cured with proper medication. There are also cases of hostile attitudes which result from hormonal disorders and can be corrected with the proper injections. There is more and more evidence that a vast number of the psychological disorders that torture people today will be treated with drugs in the future. Psychiatry is just beginning to realize the promise that it has for us. Therefore, when we experience psychological problems that do not seem to have apparent causes, such as extreme changes in attitude or intense depression, it is a good thing to turn to a psychiatrist to find out if the problem is a physical one and can be treated as such.

Second, there is *psychoanalysis*. The modern form of this therapy originated with Sigmund Freud. Psychoanalysts are those who follow in Freud's footsteps and look in the subconscious for answers to the problems which disturb people. According to the practitioners of psychoanalysis, we all have a tendency to forget or push into our subconscious minds much of what has happened to us in the past. These subconscious memories can deeply trouble us, even though we are unaware of their existence. According to psychoanalysts, our psychological troubles may be traced to such buried events in our lives. Therefore what psychoanalysts try to do through a variety of techniques is to help us remember or recover these forgotten traumas. They believe that once we gain insight into what has caused our psychological pain, we will be delivered into health and happiness. Once we understand how the forgotten events of the past have created our present unhappiness, it is assumed that those events will no longer have a destructive hold on us.

I have studied Freud and, whatever my opinion of those who have followed in the field which he created, I must admit that I believe he is one of the most profound and insightful thinkers of our times. Freud's grasp and understanding of the human personality will challenge philosophers and social scientists for generations to come, and no course in sociological or psychological theory in any university can ignore his discoveries and teachings. Freud is one of the intellectual giants of the modern era.

But despite the greatness of Sigmund Freud, I have my reservations about psychoanalysis. This is because, although Freud's diagnosis of the causes of many of our psychological maladies may be quite correct, the prescriptions he gave for delivering people from their psychological illnesses have proved relatively ineffective. When leaders of the Berlin Psychoanalytic Institute first published the cure rate of patients who came for treatment, the results were less than pleasing to Freud. As a matter of fact, he was a bit shaken and became intensely defensive when it was learned how few people had gained any long-term deliverance from their problems using his methods. In short, Freud may have understood what makes us psychological basket cases, but he did not come up with a very effective way to make us well. Insight into what ails us does not always cure us.

It seems to me that a trip into the subconscious requires great care and should not be attempted without a clear grasp of God's forgiveness and grace. What we have repressed in the past may be too painful for us to handle unless we are equipped to face it with the assurance that what we have done is forgiven by the grace of God. Those who would confront whom they really are had better be equipped by the Holy Spirit to forgive themselves. Sometimes what is to be found in the subconscious is better left repressed unless the psychotherapist is able, while guiding clients through self-discovery, to provide the assurance that there is nothing that can separate them from the love of God and that all that is discovered can be washed away. Therefore, it is necessary that all who enter the dark regions of the mind be aware of what the Bible teaches: "If we confess our sins, he is faithful and just to forgive us our sins, and to cleanse us from all unrighteousness" (1 John 1:9). Patients in psychoanalysis may find out things about themselves that will lead them to feel they cannot live with themselves any longer. And they may uncover traumas or abuse that was perpetrated upon them that drastically influences their feelings about other people. Those who would face up to the repressed ugliness of their own personal histories must do so believing: "Therefore if any man be in Christ, he is a new creature: old things are passed away; behold, all things are become new" (2 Cor. 5:17).

The third form of treatment is *psychotherapy*. This has become the most popular form of psychological help sought by troubled people and is in many respects the most questionable. Psychotherapy actually is a blanket term for a variety of treatments for emotional problems that rely primarily on talk between a trained therapist and a person seeking help. The talk aims at helping persons to become more trusting, outgoing, and able to form more stable emotional and sexual relationships. It is this "talk therapy" that most people think of when they think of psychology.

In 1952, Hans Eysenck of the University of London raised some questions about psychotherapy and gave impetus to a vast number of studies which since that time have raised doubts about the effectiveness of those who practice this cure. Eysenck's studies showed that neurotics who do *not* receive psychotherapy are just as likely to get well as those who do. Since then, some of Eysenck's research methods have been shown to be flawed. But subsequent studies which did not have the weaknesses of Eysenck's work have borne out the same conclusion that his did. Two researchers, Seymour Fisher and Roger Greenberg, both of whom are very sympathetic to psychotherapy, have more recently concluded, "There is virtually no evidence that psychotherapy generally results in more long-lasting or profound changes than other therapies."

Do not despair from these empirical findings about psychoanalyis and psychotherapy. There is hope for those who need counseling. There are professionals who can help. I know that there are people who cannot make it into the future without someone who is able to understand the sufferings of their souls. And I also know that there are godly men and women with professional training who can be effective healers for those who need help. I have no statistical evidence to make the claim that Christian counselors will succeed where their secular counterparts have failed. But this is probable: They *will* be less likely to abuse their authority and lead people away from God.

When choosing a counselor, be sure that you pick someone who will work from Christian premises and respect Christian beliefs. The counselor you choose must believe in free will. Some brands of modern psychology do not.

For instance, those who claim to be in the behaviorist school of psychology view human beings as conditioned animals who only behave as they have been trained to behave. Behaviorists do not believe that people *decide* to act. Instead, they believe that people react only in ways that have been predetermined by their past experiences.

Christians, on the other hand, believe that human beings must assume responsibility for what they do. Christians do not deny that what has happened to them in childhood influences how they look at life and how they decide. But Christians believe that every person still has a free will and ultimately decides what to do and what not to do. To choose to do what is the will of God is righteousness; to choose to do the opposite is sin. Furthermore, Christians believe that much of what is called neurosis is nothing more than the guilt and anxieties which result from transgressing the will of God.

In my own life, I have gone into deep depressions because of despicable things I have done. Those who were close to me were convinced that I needed some special psychotherapy. What I really needed to do was repent. I needed to go to the persons I had wronged and confess my sin and ask for forgiveness. I needed to lay out my life before the Lord and beg for His forgiveness and cleansing. My real need was for spiritual renewal. And I found that when I did what I had to do, I was released from the psychological burdens that had oppressed me and stolen my happiness.

O. Hobart Mowrer, the famous psychologist from the University of Illinois, contends that honest confession is the only way to emotional well-being. He does not claim to be a Christian, but he does hold to the Christian principles of counseling. He also believes that people must assume full responsibility for what they do, and that only by confessing their wrongdoings and making some kind of restitution can they find escape from the psychological torments which many of us simply call "the wages of sin." Before subjecting yourself to therapy, make sure that the counselor believes in sin and understands the need for repentance.

Joan was a friend of mine from high school days. She married and had two children. When she was thirty-six years old, she ran off with the man who lived next door to her. Her subsequent marriage fell apart, but she did not go back to her first husband and her children, even though they begged her to do so. Joan's children had a great deal of trouble while growing up, and one of them was killed in an automobile accident.

When Joan was forty-five years old, she had what might be called a nervous breakdown. After two weeks in the hospital, she was released and began a five-year process of psychotherapy. The counselor she chose was a complete secularist to whom concepts of sin and guilt were foreign. He convinced Joan that her depression was the result of things that had been done to her in her early years of childhood development. He even convinced her that she was not to blame for what had happened to her marriage.

The counselor convinced Joan that she was the innocent victim of conditioning factors that had predisposed her to be the way she was. Since she did not believe that she had sinned, she did not repent. Because she was sure that her behavior was the result of things beyond her control, she would not assume responsibility either for herself or for what had happened to her. Joan is still in therapy and probably will be for years to come. The counselor is making a lot of money. Joan has shown no signs of repentance and arrogantly looks down upon all of us "religious types" who try to tell her that she has a spiritual/moral problem with which she must deal. And Joan is still a very sick woman.

I firmly believe that any therapy that does not call us to deal with the sin in our lives is likely to be ineffective. Any therapy which does not call sinners to repentance is likely to fail. Any therapy that does not require that individuals be responsible for their actions is not Christian. In the end, good therapy always leads to a decision or a commitment. Good therapy helps the individual to set a new course for life in which God's help is sought to live out the commitments that have been made.

Another characteristic of good counseling is that the counselor helps us to believe that the goals we establish for the future can influence who and what we are in the present more than can anything that has happened to us in the past. In Christian counseling, where we have been is not as important as where we have the will to go.

As a college teacher, I have witnessed students make complete turnarounds because they have established clear and challenging goals for their lives. I have seen some of these students move from being despondent failures into being happy successes because they defined, with the help of good counseling, life goals that were desirable enough to motivate them to be diligent in their school work. I have known of marriages that have come back to life after friends and relatives thought they were dead, primarily because the partners were able to imagine a wonderful future together.

Good counseling makes us aware that we are not captives to the past but are able to live looking toward what might be, and our hopes and dreams can transform us.

Faith in the future is respected in good counseling. And the nature of that faith is brilliantly set forth in Scripture: "Now faith is the substance of things hoped for, the evidence of things not seen" (Heb. 11:1). The entire eleventh chapter of Hebrews is an account of how the great men and women of the Bible were people whose faith in what was not yet visible had sufficient power over their imaginations to motivate them to attempt great things with their lives. Good counseling does just that. It makes us believe in what we can be by the grace of God and, therefore, breaks the bonds of what we have been.

Finally, good counseling is committed to the teachings of the Word of God. For instance, I have known marriage counselors who were not committed to preserving the marriages of their clients. These counselors were primarily concerned with the happiness of their individual clients and supported the maintenance of their marriages only if those marriages were conducive to fostering that happiness. I say that you should beware of such counselors. The Bible makes a clear case for the sanctity of marriage and requires that people remain faithful mates even if this commitment appears to diminish their hopes for personal fulfillment. I am convinced that there is no lasting joy derived from violating what the Bible teaches about the obligations of marriage. Those who pursue their own happiness by leaving marriages for "something better" are usually going after pipe dreams that will lead to misery. And I believe any counseling that encourages such behavior is doing more harm than good.

There are other ways in which counseling that is not committed to biblical teaching can harm people. For instance, a particular young man was told by his counselor that the causes for his depression were related to his puritanical upbringing. His counselor told him that instead of feeling down on himself for having seduced a woman he was dating, he should become emancipated from the so-called "Victorian norms" that regulated his life. This particular young man did just that. He started into a life of promiscuity and tried to hustle into bed every woman he met. His story has not ended yet, but I cannot help but believe that this young man is headed for psychological as well as spiritual punishment.

There is help out there for those who need counseling. But when it is sought, it must be done with care. Perhaps a review of what we have covered might be helpful in choosing a counselor when one is needed:

(1) *Decide what kind of help is needed.* Perhaps your medical doctor can help you to decide whether or not your problems have physical causes. If they do, you should seek out a psychiatrist who can provide you with medication as well as counseling.

(2) *If you think that you need psychoanalysis because you feel there may be repressed memories with which you should deal, be sure that your analyst can make the grace and forgiveness of God part of your therapy.* Remember, unless we go there with Jesus and His forgiveness, there are places in our psyches where it is best for us not to go.

(3) *If you go for psychotherapy, make sure that the person to whom you go is working out of a Christian belief system*—or at very least a system that is accepting of and compatible with your beliefs. Does your psychotherapist believe that sin requires repentance and cleansing? Does he or she believe that what you hope to be with Christ's help is more important than anything in the past? Does your psychotherapist believe that prayer should be part of the therapy?

(4) *If you go for marriage counseling, be sure that your counselor puts the same premium on the preservation of marriage as the Bible does.* Make sure that he or she believes that the maintenance of a marriage is of greater value than the fulfillment of the individuals in the marriage.

(5) *Interview the person whom you are considering as a therapist.* Before you allow yourself to be that person's client, make sure that the two of you are on the same wavelength as far as religious faith is concerned. Ask the therapist or counselor what her idea of a healthy, well-adjusted Christian person is like. Find out the role that she thinks Christ should play in facilitating emotional well-being and maintaining psychological wholeness. Ask her about her philosophy of life and what part Jesus plays in it. From her answers, you can probably determine whether or not you can be in a comfortable relationship with that therapist and whether or not your therapy will help you to grow in Christ.

(6) *Do not be afraid to trust your instincts.* What you feel about the therapist or counselor may be the prompting of the Holy

Spirit. Better to be careful than sorry. Remember, the fact that the counselor is a Christian does not necessarily mean that he will be good for you. And, on the other hand, the fact that he may not be a Christian may not be sufficient reason to believe he will be bad for you. Look for somebody who will *help* you to change in ways you think you ought to change, not somebody who will try to remake you in accord with what he thinks you ought to be. You are trusting this person with your life, so caution is essential.

If you need help—get it! But be careful. A lot of psychological counseling *is* a waste of time. But the right kind of therapy can help you to become the person God intended for you to be.

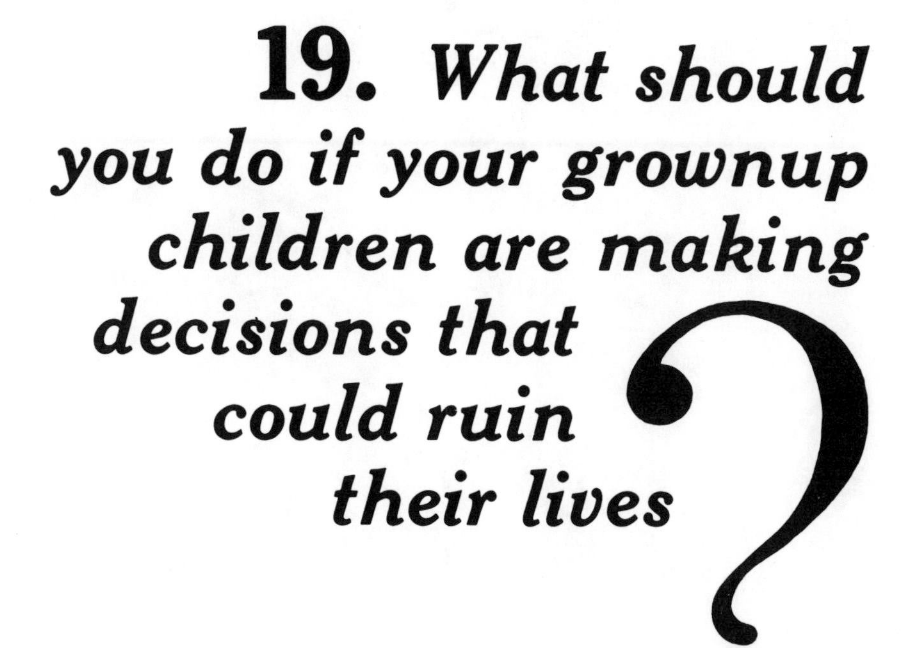

19. *What should you do if your grownup children are making decisions that could ruin their lives?*

ONE OF THE THINGS that goes with parenthood is the discovery that you no longer control your own emotions. Whether you are high with joy or down with sadness is highly contingent upon how your children are doing. If they are successful and happy, then you feel good. And if they are going through hell, then so are you.

Particularly painful are those times when your children have problems after they have grown up and are no longer under your control. You cannot order or direct the behavior of children who have become adults. Talking to them rarely helps. Often parents must helplessly endure watching their children self-destruct. How painful it is for parents from a perspective of age and greater experience to stand by with hands tied as their child makes decisions that could ruin his or her life. No sense of helplessness is more intolerable. No situation more strongly tempts parents to step into the private lives of their children and take action that can sometimes cause more harm than good.

There *are* some things parents can do in such circumstances. But they must do so with fear and trembling, because the consequences can adversely affect the parent-child relationships for years to come. Be aware that when you interfere in the life of your grownup child, there is always the strong possibility that your advice may be wrong!

Christians know that in such situations the first thing to do is to pray. However, it is usual for parents to try everything else first and then turn to prayer as a last resort. Obviously, when you pray for your children, you must not only pray that God will guide and direct *them* in all that they do; you must also pray just as hard for yourself—that God will provide clear directions as to what *you* should say and do.

But there is more to prayer than just trying to get something from God. In prayer you may find that God will do something *through* you for those who are so much on your mind and in your heart. In prayer, we usually think of getting *to* a person *through* God; we generally pray that God will convince that person of truths they seem unwilling to hear from us. So often this is the way we pray when we cannot seem to "get through" to our grownup children. But there is another possibility. I believe that those who pray can receive special power which makes them particularly effective at doing things and saying things that hitherto only resulted in failure. Persons whose previous efforts have accomplished little or nothing sometimes find that through prayer they gain the power they need to make a difference. Certainly the Bible says as much.

> And when he came to his disciples, he saw a great multitude about them, and the scribes questioning with them. And straightway all the people, when they beheld him, were greatly amazed, and running to him saluted him. And he asked the scribes, What question ye with them? And one of the multitude answered and said, Master, I have brought unto thee my son, which hath a dumb spirit; And wheresoever he taketh him, he teareth him: and he foameth, and gnasheth with his teeth, and pineth away: and I spake to thy disciples that they should cast him out; and they could not. He answereth him, and saith, O faithless generation, how long shall I be with you? how long shall I suffer you? bring him unto me. And they brought him unto him: and when he saw him, straightway the spirit tare him; and he fell on the ground, and wallowed foaming. And he asked his father, How long is it ago since this came unto him? And he said, Of a child. And oftimes it hath cast him into the fire, and into the waters, to destroy him: but if thou canst do any thing, have compassion on us, and help us. Jesus said unto him, If thou canst believe, all things are possible to him that believeth. And straightway the father of the child cried out, and said with tears, Lord, I believe; help thou mine unbelief. When Jesus saw that the people came running together, he rebuked the foul spirit, saying unto him, Thou dumb and deaf spirit, I charge thee, come out of him, and enter no more unto him. And the spirit cried, and rent him sore, and came out of him: and he was as one dead; insomuch that many said, He is dead. But Jesus took him by the hand, and lifted him up; and he arose. And when he was come into the house, his disciples asked him privately, Why could not we cast him out? And he said unto them, *This kind can come forth by nothing, but by prayer and fasting* (Mark 9:14–29, emphasis mine).

Sometimes we think that our children will be convinced to change their ways if we just use the right words and find the perfect way of phrasing our arguments. In reality, how effective we are is far more dependent upon the empowerment we receive from the Holy Spirit through prayer. The apostle Paul learned that in his ministry. He found that it was not being clever, but being spiritually empowered, that made his work effective. Paul writes to the church at Corinth:

> And I, brethren, when I came to you, came not with excellency of speech or of wisdom, declaring unto you the testimony of God. For I determined not to know any thing among you, save Jesus Christ, and him crucified. And I was with you in weakness, and in fear, and in much trembling. And my speech and my preaching was not with enticing words of man's wisdom, but in demonstration of the Spirit and of power: That your faith should not stand in the wisdom of men, but in the power of God (1 Cor. 2:1–5).

The same Jesus who died on the cross as He endured the punishment for our sins has been resurrected from the grave and is present *personally* for every person in the world. His personal presence is called the Holy Spirit. In prayer, we can experience this presence in a way that strengthens and empowers our own spirits.

When I pray, I not only ask that God do things for me; I also pray that I might feel His presence. I meditate upon Jesus. I say His name over and over again to myself. I let myself "float" in His presence. I give myself over to Him and surrender to being engulfed by Him. In that surrendered state, something can happen to me. The deadness of my heart can be taken away. A confidence that things will work together for good can be gained (Rom. 8:28). Often a sense of being empowered is experienced. After that kind of prayer, I sometimes find that I am able to reach people who were previously turned off to me and my pleadings. An old hymn writer once wrote about prayer:

> I ask no dream, no prophet ecstasies,
> No sudden rending of the veil of clay,
> No angel visitant, no opening skies;
> But take the dimness of my soul away.[1]

When the dimness of soul is removed, when the enlivening presence of God transforms me, when the power of the spirit is allowed

1. "Spirit of God, Descend Upon My Heart," attributed to George Croly, 1866.

to invade my being, I gain an effectiveness in communicating with those I love which previously was not there.

Let me share something with you that has helped me greatly. Once a week I get together with four other guys. They are special friends, and we have been meeting regularly for years. We joke, talk, read the Bible, and pray together. During these times, I sometimes experience the presence of God in a special way. There are moments when, in the context of that little group, I sense myself especially close to God and feel myself being empowered with His Spirit. On those occasions when I feel estranged from God, my friends seem able to make His presence real to me again. When I do not seem able to make contact with that ultimate source of spiritual power, it is then that they become conduits through whom the power once again begins to flow into my life. I suggest that if you feel unable to gain the power to be what you should be for those whom you love, start meeting regularly with a small group of fellow believers and, in fellowship with them, discover the power that seems lacking.

> Again I say unto you, That if two of you shall agree on earth as touching any thing that they shall ask, it shall be done for them of my Father which is in heaven. For where two or three are gathered together in my name, there am I in the midst of them (Matt. 18:19–20).

You will find that when you are empowered with the Spirit, you have something special going for you. You may find that you do not have to say anything at all, that instead something goes out from you that touches your children in ways your worn-out arguments never could. Your children have probably heard or thought of everything you could possibly say, anyway. But often they are not prepared for that soft, sweet, but nevertheless, overpowering presence of God that you communicate when you come equipped with prayer. Cynics might call it some kind of mental telepathy or a version of ESP. Call it anything you choose. All I know is that there is a communication in the Spirit that does not require words and which words can never communicate. In those times when words would only make matters worse, communication through the power of the Spirit is all that we can bring to our adult sons and daughters.

Prayer is the ultimate means of reaching grownup children, but most of us feel we must also tell them what we are thinking. For your own peace of mind, letting your children know what you fear for them in the actions they are taking is sometimes a necessity. Perhaps you need to feel that you have done all that you could to prevent the trouble that you expect. Perhaps you want to be sure that your children do not come back to you someday asking, "Why didn't you tell me what you thought? Maybe I would have listened." If you do decide that you must speak to your children, there are some things to bear in mind.

First, realize that you will have to live with what you say for years to come. I know a woman who was sure that her son was about to marry someone who would ruin his life. And there was indeed much about her son's prospective wife that most mothers would find objectionable. The young woman had lived a very loose life. She had been married before and had borne a child out of wedlock. The mother knew that her son, who was not exactly the prize his mother thought he was, had picked her up at a bar. The prospective daughter-in-law was indeed a puritan mother's nightmare.

The mother confronted her son with her concerns. Unfortunately, she was neither diplomatic nor kind. She labeled her future daughter-in-law in ways that would serve as barriers to her ever being friends with the young woman—barring a miracle. Her son married the woman he had chosen anyway. And eventually that wayward woman straightened herself out. While she did not become a Christian, she has adopted a fairly decent lifestyle. Unfortunately, the words of that mother to her son created such a bad situation that to this day she has not been invited to her son's home nor been allowed to get to know her three grandchildren.

Remember the words of the apostle James:

> Behold, we put bits in the horses' mouths, that they may obey us; and we turn about their whole body. Behold also the ships, which though they be so great, and are driven of fierce winds, yet are they turned about with a very small helm, whithersoever the governor listeth. Even so the tongue is a little member, and boasteth great things. Behold, how great a matter a little fire kindleth! And the tongue is a fire, a world of iniquity: so is the tongue among our members, that it defileth the whole body, and setteth on fire the course of nature; and it is set on fire of hell. For every kind of

> beasts, and of birds, and of serpents, and of things in the sea, is tamed, and hath been tamed of mankind: But the tongue can no man tame; it is an unruly evil, full of deadly poison (James 3:3–8).

Do not question this scripture! If you are going to say anything to your children about the decisions they are making, you must pray hard to keep from saying things that may be painfully destructive. You need restraint which only God can provide. You lack the discipline to keep from saying the wrong thing. There must be a special leaning on the Lord to prevent you from saying things that could haunt you for a lifetime. Words once spoken cannot be taken back, no matter how much you may regret them later. It is best to say less than you might and then, if necessary, say more another day.

The second thing to remember in talking to your grown children is: Do not make threats. Do not say things like, "If you do that I never want you in this house again" or "I'll never speak to you again." How many people do you know who are permanently cut off from members of their families because of such ultimatums or threats? Whatever you say must be said in such a way that the door is left open for your children. You must leave them with a strong sense that they will always be loved, no matter what they do. You must communicate, *without saying it,* that though you may be hurt by what they do, you will always love them and welcome whomever they marry as though that person were your own flesh and blood. Never burn bridges. Never try to blackmail your children into doing your will with threats of cutting them off. In short, never say never.

It would be well for you to read the story of the prodigal son before you take any action at all:

> And he said, A certain man had two sons: And the younger of them said to his father, Father, give me the portion of goods that falleth to me. And he divided unto them his living. And not many days after the younger son gathered all together, and took his journey into a far country, and there wasted his substance with riotous living. And when he had spent all, there arose a mighty famine in that land; and he began to be in want. And he went and joined himself to a citizen of that country; and he sent him into his field to feed swine. And he would fain have filled his belly with the husks that the swine did eat: and no man gave unto him. And when he came to himself, he said, How many hired servants of my father's have bread enough and to

> spare, and I perish with hunger! I will arise and go to my father, and will say unto him, Father, I have sinned against heaven, and before thee, and am no more worthy to be called thy son: make me as one of thy hired servants. And he arose, and came to his father. But when he was yet a great way off, his father saw him, and had compassion, and ran, and fell on his neck, and kissed him. And the son said unto him, Father, I have sinned against heaven, and in thy sight, and am no more worthy to be called thy son. But the father said to his servants, Bring forth the best robe, and put it on him; and put a ring on his hand, and shoes on his feet: And bring hither the fatted calf, and kill it; and let us eat, and be merry: For this my son was dead, and is alive again: he was lost, and is found. And they began to be merry (Luke 15:11–24).

In this story, the father was well aware of the fact that his son was making a wrong decision. He knew that if his son left home with half of the family's fortune, the boy would come to no good. But there were no threats. And after the son left home, the door was always open for his return—and he knew it. There was a long wait for the son's return, but the father, like our Heavenly Father, had unlimited patience and love. And when the son did return, his father ran out to meet him. The boy did not have to humiliate himself or come crawling before his father would accept him. There was no "I told you so!" attitude on the part of the father. There was no recrimination. There was only the warm welcome of a loving father who had waited a long time for his son's return. That father is a model for every parent whose son or daughter is making potentially ruinous decisions. If children persist in wrecking their lives, parents must be waiting to pick up the pieces and put them back together again. One prominent American author has said, "Home is the place where, when you have to go there, they have to take you in." The children of Christian parents should always be able to come home.

Monica, the mother of St. Augustine, prayed for a long time for the salvation of her worldly son. Augustine's life was a moral disaster, and his mother wept often for her despicable son. One day Augustine told his mother that he had made a decision to go from Hippo, the city in North Africa where they lived, to Rome. Monica was sure that in Rome her son would be completely destroyed. She was convinced that in that sin capital of the world her dear boy would be consumed by the desires of the flesh.

Upon hearing of Augustine's decision, Monica pled with him to accompany her to church and pray with her about his decision. He went, but while she was on her knees praying for God to change her son's mind, Augustine seized the opportunity to sneak out of the church, hurry to the dock, and board the ship that would take him to Rome. When his mother rose from her knees, Augustine was gone.

There are many who in such a situation would feel not only emotionally crushed, but also deserted by God. There are some who might even stop believing in God altogether. But Monica hung in there and continued to patiently hold up her son in prayer.

While in Rome, Augustine did the expected. He lived in sin and behaved like a libertine. But unexpectedly one day, seemingly out of nowhere, he heard a voice say, "Take and read." This led him to read the Scripture and to become a Christian. Under the direction of St. Ambrose, Augustine grew in faith. Eventually he was appointed bishop of the church of Hippo. His mother was at the dock waiting with the other members of the church for the arrival of the new pastor of their church. Can you imagine her surprise and joy when Augustine stepped off the ship? Monica's prayers had been answered beyond her wildest anticipation.

In the words of that baseball philosopher, Yogi Berra, "It's not over 'till it's over." If being a parent is anything, it is patience and an unwillingness to give up on your children no matter what.

A third point to remember in talking to your children: Say what you have to say once and with sufficient clarity and emphasis so that you do not have to bring it up over and over again. It is a good idea to set up a special time to discuss the matter. If you wait for the perfect time to arise, it probably never will.

When I have something of utmost importance that I want to say to either of my grownup children, I set up a special time to see them. Perhaps I might arrange for us to meet for lunch. I make sure that we have ample time so that any discussion is not rushed. Generally I choose a public restaurant because the surroundings force us to handle our concerns in hushed tones. (For people with Italian temperaments this is a very good idea.) Furthermore, I find that we are able to handle things better in the relaxed conditions created by a good meal. I try to be direct, and I lay out everything I have to say. I listen to my child's response with care. I share what I believe the Bible has to say about the matter at hand. (I have prepared for this with careful study of Scripture before we get together.) I make sure the discussion does not drag on. I end our discussion by asking for a decision to be made. (All good encounters have what can be called "closure.") I want to come away knowing what my child thinks of what I have said and what he or she plans to do in light of that.

When we are done, we are done. I do not bring up the matter again unless I am asked to do so. It is a mistake to have children duck every time they meet you because they are afraid you are going to sing the same old song over and over again. Say what has to be said forcefully, with love and without slander. Then drop the matter unless you are requested to talk about it later on. If your child does ask you to deal with it again, it would be wise to repeat this same process and plan.

Finally, be ready to accept what cannot be changed. Learn to pray the well-known and much-loved Serenity Prayer:

> God, grant me the serenity to accept the things I cannot change,
> The courage to change the things I can,
> And the wisdom to know the difference.

If things do not turn out the way you had hoped, do not feel guilty. I am convinced that when our children do what is good, parents take too much credit. And when children do what is wrong, parents take too much blame. Children are autonomous creatures with wills of their own. Remember, God created two perfect children (Adam and Eve), set them in a perfect environment, and both of them ended up rebelling against Him. Those people who upon learning of someone else's grownup child gone wrong, piously chirp, "Train up a child in the way he should go: and when he is old, he will not depart from it," (Prov. 22:6) probably never had any children of their own.

Remember, Jesus could not reach some of the members of His own family. From the Scriptures and from church historians we learn that He had some brothers who acknowledged Him as Lord and Savior, and He had other brothers who rejected Him. The fact that people grow up in a home where godly influences abound is no guarantee that everything will turn out as we might hope. We are assured that God's grace will carry you through all your disappointments. He is sufficient in time of trouble.

20. *Are evangelicals too pro-Israel?*

OVER THE CENTURIES, persecution has been the constant lot of the Jews as they have tried to make their homes among the peoples of the world. They were persecuted in Spain during the Inquisition, and they were declared guilty of the death of Christ by the Roman Catholic clergy for almost fifteen hundred years. They were uprooted and displaced in Russia, hounded into substandard living conditions in Poland, unjustly persecuted in England, and rendered second-class citizens in other countries. All through the Western world, hatred for the Jews has simmered, waiting to express itself.

We all know what happened to the Jews in Germany during the days of the Third Reich. What is not as widely known is the role our own nation, the United States, played in creating the Holocaust.

Little is said or written about the fact that when the Jews sought to flee Nazi Germany in the late 1930s, the immigration laws of our country generated by the racist Loughlin Report of the United States Congress and by the white supremacist theory outlined in Madison Grant's *The Passing of the Great White Race* led to the prohibiting of the entrance of Jews into the land of the free and the home of the brave.

Little is said about the conference called by Winston Churchill to address the need for new homes for Jewish refugees, because at that conference President Franklin D. Roosevelt consented to admitting into America only a few thousand homeless Jews, while suggesting that others might find a place to live in the impoverished Dominican Republic. We make sure that little is included in our school children's textbooks to inform them that thousands of Jewish refugees who sailed to our country and begged for sanctuary encountered immigration officials in New York Harbor who forced their ships to return to Germany, where many of them faced death.

Most of us know the famous words of Emma Lazarus inscribed on the base of the Statue of Liberty:

Give me your tired, your poor,
Your huddled masses yearning to breathe free,
The wretched refuse of your teeming shore.
Send them, the homeless, the tempest-tossed to me:
I lift up my lamp beside the golden door.

But few of us realize that these words only mocked thousands of Jews who sought refuge from persecution among us. The prejudices of the White, Anglo-Saxon, Protestant establishment of America again were responsible for policies that left many Jews with no alternative other than to try to make the best of living in Nazi territories. Eventually, most of them were put to death.

Anti-Semitism is a disease of Western Christian nations. It is *our* malady. It is *our* psychosis.

I believe that it was anti-Semitism that provided much of the motivation among Western nations to create the state of Israel. The efforts of Zionists notwithstanding, the state of Israel exists today largely because Western nations saw that the easiest solution to "the Jewish problem" was to "dump" unwanted Jews onto Arab land.

The fact that Arab peoples would be displaced and turned into refugees because of this plan did not bother us. We turned our heads and pretended not to see the injustices endured by the Palestinian people as they had their homeland taken away from them by strangers. No matter that they had farmed the land for almost two millenia. No matter that they lost this land through the intrigue and betrayal of the British government, as evidenced by the infamous Sykes-Picot Agreement of 1916. (No matter that even now, thousands of Arabs are being displaced by the building of new Israeli settlements on the "occupied territory" of Palestine.) All that mattered was that "the Jewish problem" appeared solved.

The politicians who created the state of Israel got some unexpected support from the evangelical community. There were many among us who believed the Bible teaches that prior to the second coming of Christ the people of Israel must return to their homeland. There was, and is even today among most evangelicals, a common acceptance that the second coming of Christ necessitates that the Jews occupy Jerusalem and rebuild their temple on Mount Zion. Thus, when the state of Israel was created and the Jews began to return to Palestine, most evangelicals cheered.

Our interpretation of Bible prophecies made us into enthusiastic supporters of policies that led to the displacement of Palestinians with little regard to the injustices they suffered.

And this is still true today. We pity Palestinian refugees. Compassion even motivates us to make financial contributions to further missionary work among them. But we demonstrate little commitment to social justice on their behalf. How can we expect to win our Arab brothers and sisters to Christ when our interpretation of the Scriptures calls for an unjust assessment of their rights to land that was held by their fathers for centuries?

Whether the Jewish people should or should not be in Israel is now only an academic question to many of us. They are there. They will remain there, and the other nations of the world are left with no alternative but to guarantee the right of the state of Israel to exist. At this stage of history, the United States must commit itself to the survival of the state of Israel. As Christians, we should even rejoice that our Jewish brothers and sisters have a homeland that assures them of an identity and dignity hitherto impossible.

On the other hand, I believe we must urge our Jewish friends to do for others what they would have others do for them. They, more than any other people on the planet, must understand the hunger of the Palestinians for a homeland of their own. There will be no peace in the Middle East until there is a Palestinian homeland and, like it or not, there will be no peace in the Middle East until there are negotiations with the Palestine Liberation Organization. I believe that we, as Christians, should urge our Jewish brothers and sisters to see the justice of resolving the problems of the Middle East by turning the Gaza Strip and the West Bank into a Palestinian state.

Arabs can learn to live with Jews. They have said as much. They are not anti-Semitic. As an Arab statesman correctly said to me:

> Do not call Arabs anti-Semitic.
> We, ourselves, are Semitic people.
> The Jews are our blood cousins through Abraham.
> It is you Christians who are anti-Semitic.
> You are the ones who do not want Jews for neighbors.
> You are the ones who do not want Jews as business partners.
> You are the ones who drive them from your midst.

> You are the ones who have tried to murder them all.
> And when you could not kill them,
> You stole our land and placed them where they are to live.
> And when we objected to the loss of our homeland,
> You had the audacity to call us anti-Semitic.

I have heard some opponents to the Palestinian cause claim that there is no need to establish a homeland for Palestinians because they are not a distinct people with a clear national identity. The argument these opponents offer is that the so-called Palestinians are really only displaced Jordanians, which Jordan ought to assimilate, and some nomads who have no national identity at all.

Such arguments, I believe, ignore the sociological factors which create nations and the conditions which give identity to a particular people. In times past, it has been adversity that has given birth to nations. It has been oppression that has caused people to realize they have a common destiny in which their life chances depend upon their being committed to each other. There sometimes comes a moment when struggling people, say, in the words of Benjamin Franklin, "We must all hang together, or surely we will all hang separately." At such a moment, the collective consciousness which we call a nation comes into being.

There is a nation called Palestine because, for the people on the West Bank and in the Gaza strip, pressures exerted by Israel have helped to create it. The prejudice and second-class citizenship which the Palestinian people have had to endure since they became refugees following the Six Day War have made them into a distinct people, and they now want a land they can call their own.

Evangelicals have supported the creation of the state of Israel. Now justice requires that we support the creation of a homeland for Palestinians. For this to be accomplished, we must convince our Jewish brothers and sisters that we Christians do not support their denial of Palestinian hopes for a nation of their own.

In addition, we must call upon our Arab brothers and sisters to recognize the facts of history—to accept the existence of the state of Israel and guarantee the integrity of its borders. They must be made to realize that Israel is here to stay.

Finally, we must show both our Arab and Jewish friends that our understanding of the Bible does not commit us to a Middle

East policy necessitating that the Jews occupy Jerusalem as a prior condition to the second coming of our Lord, and that Jews and Arabs, so far as we are concerned, can jointly share in control of the Holy City.

Personally, I have some difficulty with the interpretation of Scripture that requires that Jews be the sole possessors of Palestine as a precondition to the return of Christ. To hold such a belief would render foolish all those Christians who looked for the second coming of Christ prior to 1948 (when the state of Israel was created). Furthermore, to hold that the Temple of Jerusalem must be rebuilt before the Lord can come back to earth again would make Paul's admonition to the ancient church at Thessalonica absurd (see 1 Thess. 4:13–5:6). Why should they have been instructed to look for the coming of the Lord prior to the events that have transpired since 1948 if those events did indeed have to take place before the Lord's coming?

Jesus told His disciples that their generation would not pass away before everything that needed to be fulfilled for His return would take place. I do not believe that the Lord was wrong. I am convinced that by A.D. 70 everything was in place for the return of Christ, and that it has been right for Christians to expect His return ever since that time. There is no need for evangelicals to advocate unjust policies in the Middle East on the supposition that land must be taken from the Arabs and given to the Jews in order to create the conditions essential for the return of Christ.

I know that my viewpoint is controversial, but I must point out that for centuries Christians did not see any need for the restoration of the state of Israel or the rebuilding of the temple as a precondition for the return of Christ. From the day of Pentecost until the present, Christians have always lived in the immediate expectancy that the Lord could return. I believe they were not wrong.

In my opinion, evangelicals must be pro-Israel, but they must also be pro-justice for Arabs. Christians, Muslims, and Jews must find a way that will enable us all to live together in love and friendship. Biblical justice requires that we commit ourselves every bit as much to establishing a home for refugee Palestinians as we were committed to creating the state of Israel for refugee Jews. While the Bible says that those who bless Israel will be blessed, it also reminds us that those who do not pursue justice will be cursed.

> Woe unto him that buildeth his house by unrighteousness, and his chambers by wrong; that useth his neighbour's service without wages, and giveth him not for his work; that saith, I will build me a wide house and large chambers, and cutteth him out windows; and it is cieled with cedar, and painted with vermilion. Shalt thou reign, because thou closest thyself in cedar? did not thy father eat and drink, and do judgment and justice, and then it was well with him? He judged the cause of the poor and needy; then it was well with him; was not this to know me? saith the Lord (Jer. 22:13–16).

A postscript

TOO OFTEN, when all is said and done, it has been mostly *said.* I hope that what I have tried to say in this book will do more than just stimulate discussion and controversy. I hope that it will create changes in lifestyles. The chapters of this book are not meant to be a set of academic treatises, but a series of important questions that require readers to answer with action, not with intellectual agreement. Dialogue is important, but we must do more than talk about these heavy issues.

I believe that the time is ripe for significant changes in our lives and in our world. I believe that single people ought to consider ending their loneliness by living in community. I am convinced that parents must reconsider the value of traditional patterns for rearing children. It is my prayer that Christians will turn from the homophobia that has led to the persecution of gay people and discover new ways to express love to these hurting brothers and sisters. I think we must find ways to care for the elderly and to enable them to live and die with dignity. I believe that faithfulness to the Sermon on the Mount requires that we take a new look at radical living and dare to reject militarism and the affluent American lifestyle. In all of these matters, I want the Bible to be our guide. I pray that I have been faithful to the Bible in what I have written.